UNDERSTANDING & USING RESEARCH IN SOCIAL WORK

SAGE was founded in 1965 by Sara Miller McCune to support
the dissemination of usable knowledge by publishing innovative
and high-quality research and teaching content. Today, we
publish more than 850 journals, including those of more than
300 learned societies, more than 800 new books per year, and
a growing range of library products including archives, data,
case studies, reports, and video. SAGE remains majority-owned
by our founder, and after Sara's lifetime will become owned by
a charitable trust that secures our continued independence.

Los Angeles | London | New Delhi | Singapore | Washington DC

UNDERSTANDING & USING RESEARCH IN SOCIAL WORK

BRIAN J. TAYLOR, CAMPBELL KILLICK & ANNE MCGLADE

MASTERING Social Work Practice

Los Angeles | London | New Delhi
Singapore | Washington DC

Learning Matters
An imprint of SAGE Publications Ltd
1 Oliver's Yard
55 City Road
London EC1Y 1SP

SAGE Publications Inc.
2455 Teller Road
Thousand Oaks, California 91320

SAGE Publications India Pvt Ltd
B 1/I 1 Mohan Cooperative Industrial Area
Mathura Road
New Delhi 110 044

SAGE Publications Asia-Pacific Pte Ltd
3 Church Street
#10-04 Samsung Hub
Singapore 049483

Editor: Kate Wharton
Development editor: Lauren Simpson
Production editor: Chris Marke
Copy editor: Diana Chambers
Proofreader: Sue Edwards
Marketing manager: Tamara Navaratnam
Cover design: Wendy Scott
Typeset by: C&M Digitals (P) Ltd, Chennai, India

Library of Congress Control Number: 2015946647

British Library Cataloguing in Publication Data

A catalogue record for this book is available from the British Library

ISBN: 978-1-4739-0814-7 (pbk)
ISBN: 978-1-4739-0813-0 (hbk)

Contents

About the authors

Brian Taylor is Professor of Social Work at Ulster University in Northern Ireland where he has the lead role for research in social work. He spent ten years in practice and fifteen years in professional training and organisation development in social work before moving to the university. He teaches research methods to Ph.D. students and to experienced social workers undertaking postgraduate, post-qualifying study. He was module coordinator for an innovative Introduction to Evidence Based Practice module on the B.Sc. qualifying social work programme. Brian leads the university social work research cluster on Decision, Assessment, Risk and Evidence Studies and is the primary organiser of a biennial international symposium on this topic. He was a member of the Cross-Border Child Protection Research and Knowledge Transfer Sub-Committee of the North–South Ministerial Council for the island of Ireland. Brian is an honorary Senior Fellow of the School for Social Care Research of the National Institute for Health Research, London.

Campbell Killick is employed as a Research Officer (Social Work) within a Health and Social Care Trust in Northern Ireland. This innovative post allows him to support practitioners to use research findings and participate in research activity. Campbell's social work background includes disability and mental health, and he is involved in training relating to the safeguarding of adults and children. Campbell's Ph.D. was on the topic of professional decision making in adult protection, and his research interests include professional decision making, assessment processes and the use of evidence in practice.

Anne Glade has been Social Care Research Lead for the Social Care and Children's Directorate, Health and Social Care Board since October 2013. She is the lead on the development of the Research and Continuous Improvement Strategy (2015–2020) In Pursuit of Excellence in Evidence Informed Social Work Services in Northern Ireland. She has a long-standing career working in research and evaluation research in health and social care and other settings in England and Northern Ireland. She has a keen interest in the needs of older people, people with disabilities and people from black and minority ethnic groups. She has undertaken and published a range of research studies in these areas. Her interest in equality and human rights led to a career spanning a number of years as an adviser to a range of health and social care organisations.

She is also a visiting lecturer and co-tutor on two post-qualifying programmes for social workers at Ulster University: the Application of Research Methods in Social Work and the Evidence Informed Professional and Organisation.

Acknowledgements

We would like to thank Janice McQuilkin, Joanne Knox (Assistant Librarians) and Niall Burns (Librarian) at Ulster University, who have worked with us over the past decade and have helped hundreds of social work students to develop knowledge and skills in retrieving research relevant to social work topics. We would like to thank the undergraduate (qualifying programme) and postgraduate (post-qualifying programme) social work students for their collaboration in 'road testing' various ideas and materials contained here. In particular, we would like to thank the experienced social workers who have undertaken the Research Methods Programme, post-qualifying M.Sc. dissertation module provided by Ulster University and employer partners, and also our fellow tutors and practice assessors on this programme. Their experiences and reflections have greatly enriched our understanding. Thanks to Mabel Stevenson, Research Assistant at Ulster University who so willingly assisted with some visual material and tidying references.

Chapter 1

Introduction

This introductory chapter outlines the context in which this book has been written in terms of the audience, the profession and the experience of the authors. It identifies the need for the book in its policy and service context. This introduction outlines the chapters of the book and how they are sequenced and relate to each other, and concludes with notes on terminology and the scope of the book.

In an increasingly information-rich society we all – as citizens, as providers of services and as users of services – need skills to evaluate the data and knowledge available to us. This challenge applies particularly to the understanding and use of research by professionals – the focus of this book. Although there is a challenge in undertaking worthwhile and robust research in social work, this book focuses on the wider challenge that faces a much larger number of professionals – namely, understanding and using research to inform practice rather than undertaking research. What is required by all professionals is an ability to confidently shape a question that might be answered by research, identify relevant studies to address the question and have some idea about appraising the quality of that research. Professionals need skills in synthesising studies and presenting this summary coherently to colleagues in terms of its implications for their practice. In short, all social workers – like all other professionals – require the knowledge and skills necessary to be evidence-informed professionals and to participate in evidence-informed organisations. That is the focus of this book.

This book is an introduction to a key dimension of accountable, reflective, professional practice in social work. The book aims to support the development of reflective practice by focusing on the use of knowledge from research to inform practice. The focus is on the knowledge and skills required to access, appraise, synthesise and use research, in the context of understanding the challenges to using knowledge to inform professional practice. This book will support the development of knowledge and skills that are transferable across client groups and settings. It will be a valuable text for any student in social work undertaking a project or case study where they need to identify relevant research, present some appraisal of that research, and show some application to the client(s) or situation in the case study or project.

The need for the book

The development of effective interventions to help other human beings in need lies at the heart of social work practice. Social work is not just an academic discipline studying people, their needs or the impact of government policies, but is primarily a professional discipline committed to using the most effective psychosocial interventions to help individuals, families, groups and communities to better their lives, safeguard those who are vulnerable to abuse or serious harm, and contribute to protecting citizens from the harmful effects of crime. Social work intervenes to reduce the likelihood of harm, stimulate self-help, provide therapeutic interventions, safeguard those at greatest risk, and enhance and maintain – or at least reduce deterioration of – functional abilities. The focus of social work is on intentional, planned intervention to help people achieve beneficial change.

It is imperative that the social work profession gets to grips with the issue of demonstrating that its interventions are effective, challenging though this may be. The birth of the profession of social work lies precisely in the fact that we are not merely helping people out of the goodness that is in our hearts, but that what we do is effective enough to merit being funded by society, whether through charitable giving or tax-payer funding. Calls to demonstrate this effectiveness go back to the beginnings of social work as a distinct occupation:

> I appeal to you, measure, evaluate, estimate, and appraise your results in some form, in any terms that rest on anything beyond faith, assertion and the 'illustrative case'. Let us do this for ourselves before some less knowledgeable and less gentle body takes us by the shoulders and pushes us out into the streets.

> (Cabot, 1931, p6, quoted in Sheldon et al., 2005, p12)

From these beginnings have grown diverse efforts within the profession to create and use evidence about 'what works', involving also understanding why 'it' works. This in turn raises questions about how recipients view interventions, accessibility of services and related questions. Much social work activity is funded by governments, and increasingly decisions about public funding of services demand some explicit evidence base. Voluntary and private sector organisations also increasingly require more transparent argument where major decisions are involved. A recent example in England was the selection of a counselling method to address low-level mental health problems (Department of Health, 2001). On the basis of the argument – using research as primary evidence – a particular counselling method (cognitive behavioural therapy) was selected for the investment of considerable public funding. The call for social work to be more mindful of a useful evidence base has been repeated increasingly in recent years:

> When professionals intervene in people's lives they should do so on the basis of the best available evidence regarding the likely consequences of their actions. Put simply, they should be as confident as possible that what they do will (1) bring about the changes sought, and (2) will do so without adverse consequences

> (Macdonald, 2008, p435)

Within purely academic subjects, many types of questions may be asked and answers sought. For any profession, questions about effectiveness are central because the purpose of a profession is to deliver an (effective) service within society. Distinct types of questions need to be asked in order to develop effective interventions, and different types of research method tend to be best suited to addressing different types of question. This book addresses the knowledge and skills required to understand various stages of developing and evaluating complex interventions, such as those carried out by social workers (Medical Research Council, 2008). We present surveys as primarily addressing questions about prevalence (such as of problems faced by individuals and families in society) and correlations between factors in their environment so as to inform our understandings of needs and strengths. We present qualitative studies as primarily helping to shape the concepts and understandings required to design interventions, and to understand the experiences of people receiving and providing services so that processes might be improved. We present experimental and quasi-experimental studies as primarily seeking to measure the effectiveness of interventions by excluding alternative explanations for change.

In this book we discuss briefly the debates about the terms 'evidence-based practice' (EBP) and 'evidence-informed practice' (EIP), and have gone on to focus our attention on the practical real-world issues of using research so as to improve the services we offer. Where we use these terms we are working approximately to the definitions below.

- Evidence-based practice is the term used internationally and across professions and organisations to refer to basing professional judgements and service decisions on the best evidence available at that time, focusing primarily on knowledge gained from generalisable, robust research.

- Evidence-informed practice is a term used by people concerned that the term evidence-based practice might imply a particular process of establishing evidence, a defined prioritisation of research designs regardless of research question, or a neglect of other sources of knowledge that are required for professional practice.

The focus of this book is on understanding and using research – and also service evaluations and professional audit which are related sources of knowledge – to inform practice. Reflective practice in general is beyond the scope of this book and the interested reader is referred to Darragh and Taylor (2008).

The audience for the book

This book is written for student social workers towards the end of their qualifying training and for qualified social workers undertaking projects and post-qualifying studies. The book will support professionals undertaking post-qualifying studies needing knowledge and skills in identifying, understanding and using research, and doctoral students in social work in their literature reviewing. In particular, the book will support senior practitioners who need the knowledge and skills to ensure that they can keep abreast of developments in their own field, and remain champions for their area of practice and responsibility. Academically, our main pitch has been at postgraduate (Master's) level, although the material is presented in such a way that undergraduates and doctoral students can use the knowledge and skills in varying depth appropriate to the level required.

The book will also be of interest to professionals from a range of disciplines, particularly in healthcare, where similar principles and methods for understanding and using research also apply. Although we recognise that all workers in the social care field should seek to base their practice on a sound knowledge base, the focus of this book is on social workers on the premise that professional accountability carries with it an obligation to maintain public confidence through continuing professional development (CPD) and use of research to inform practice and policy decisions (Taylor et al., 2010). In increasing numbers of countries, evidence of CPD is required for continuing registration as a social worker, and therefore required in order to continue to practise.

This book is based on over a decade of work by the team of authors in supervising research projects and teaching research methods to experienced social workers undertaking post-qualifying, postgraduate studies. The text is also informed by a decade of providing a module on evidence-based practice to final year students on qualifying (undergraduate) social work programmes; by teaching research methods to Ph.D. students across all academic disciplines; and by involvement in rigorous systematic reviewing as part of the Cochrane Collaboration. This experience of teaching the topic across a range of levels of knowledge and experience has provided a sound framework for pitching this book at an appropriate level while also connecting with a wider audience.

This book focuses on professionals understanding and using research to inform service improvement. As noted above, research of various types is required in order to create, develop and evaluate effective interventions. Research use is being seen increasingly as an aspect of social care governance (Taylor and Campbell, 2011). For example, research might inform judgements about types of outcomes that one might expect clients typically to achieve as a result of a particular intervention. In practice, much research evidence reaches the 'front line' through assessment tools (e.g. Taylor, 2012b). In this context, the knowledge and skills in this book should assist the reader in contributing to developing and appraising assessment tools for practice in terms of their evidence base.

Meeting professional standards

England

In this book, links are made to the relevant requirements of the Professional Capabilities Framework (PCF) for Social Workers in England to facilitate students studying for a professional social work degree in England to make connections between this material and their professional development (see Appendix 5).

The PCF is an overarching professional standards framework for social work in England which aims to:

- set out consistent expectations of social workers at every stage in their career;
- provide a backdrop to initial social work education and continuing professional development after qualification;
- inform the design and implementation of the national career structure; and
- give social workers a framework around which to plan their careers and professional development.

The PCF has nine career levels spanning:

1. entry level (social work students);
2. readiness for direct practice;
3. end of first placement;
4. end of last placement;
5. readiness for direct practice (NQSW/ASYE);
6. social worker;
7. experienced social worker;
8. advanced level; and
9. strategic level.

The PCF has nine domains which focus on specific areas of practice. This book relates particularly to *Domain 5: Knowledge*, including the need to:

5.1   Demonstrate a comprehensive understanding and use of knowledge related to your area of practice, including critical awareness of current issues and new evidence based practice research.

5.10 Recognise the contribution, and begin to make use, of research to inform practice.

5.11 Demonstrate a critical understanding of research methods.

The PCF is owned by The College of Social Work in England and is available at: www. tcsw.org.uk/ProfessionalCapabilitiesFramework/.

Scotland, Wales and Northern Ireland

For Scotland, Wales and Northern Ireland the National Occupational Standards for Social Work and post-qualifying frameworks are a valuable point of reference.

- National Occupational Standards for Social Work:

  www.ccwales.org.uk/national-occupational-standards/

- Northern Ireland Professional in Practice (post-qualifying) Framework:

  www.niscc.info/index.php/education-for-our-training-providers/social-work-professional-development-pq

- Scottish Post-Qualifying Framework:

  www.sssc.uk.com/about-the-sssc/multimedia-library/publications/70-education-and-training/post-qualifying-social-work-learning-and-development-in-scotland-2014

- Welsh Post-Qualifying Framework:

  www.ccwales.org.uk/post-qualifying-training/

For Northern Ireland, this book is written particularly to support the development of the knowledge and skills necessary to put into effect the Social Work Research Strategy (Health and Social Care Board, 2015). These frameworks help to give the academic discipline of social work its coherence and identity, and define what can be expected of a graduate in terms of knowledge and skills for competent practice. For other professions and for social workers in other countries, the knowledge and skills taught here will be readily transferable.

In the UK the Social Care Institute for Excellence (SCIE) aims to improve the lives of people who use care services by sharing knowledge about what works. This initiative emphasises the need for research to underpin sound practice (Marsh & Fisher, 2005; Shaw et al., 2004). SCIE has pioneered the development of evidence-based practice: seeking ways to bring research knowledge closer to practitioners. The early work by Jennie Popay and Katrina Roen (2003) on methods of synthesising research has been developed through the guidance on **systematic reviews** of Esther Coren and Mike Fisher (2006) through to a more polished guidance document (Rutter et al., 2010). All professionals need to be able to understand and use research; only a few within each profession require the knowledge and skills to carry out research (Campbell et al., 2016).

The need for systematic approaches to reviewing the best available evidence (Macdonald, 2003) sets the scene for the practical knowledge and skills outlined in this book. Robust studies of the effectiveness of social work interventions have come a long way in the past decades. The Cochrane Collaboration (see Further Reading, below) provides a library which contains systematic reviews of the effectiveness of more than seventy interventions that might be carried out or commissioned by professional social workers. Reviews of the effectiveness of a wide range of social welfare interventions are in the library of the Campbell Collaboration (see Further Reading). We have borne these and the principles in the SCIE guidance on systematic reviewing in mind, although our target audience is social workers and social work students on Bachelor's, Master's and doctoral degree programmes carrying out less rigorous reviews of best evidence than these. For a Ph.D., the literature review should be publishable as a journal article in its own right. This depends essentially on the degree of methodological rigour used in the process, and this book will assist with the essential knowledge and skills required.

The Economic and Social Research Council, the main funding body for social work research in the UK, has identified that we need *a fundamental step change in breadth, depth and quality of the UK research base in social work and social care* (ESRC, 2008, p1). This recognition has led to a funded initiative to develop the teaching on **quantitative research** methods on qualifying social work training. This book aims to support this initiative with readily accessible material relevant to social work on research quality.

There is also an impetus towards more effective use of research from case law in England about professional negligence. The traditional standard in the UK was that a professional was not guilty of negligence if he or she had acted in accordance with a practice accepted as proper by a responsible body of professionals skilled in that particular art (see Mr Justice McNair's direction to the jury in *Bolam v Friern Hospital Management Committee* [1957]). A more recent judgment sets a higher standard, that also professionals must be able to give a rationale such as research evidence or a theoretical basis for their views if challenged (*Bolitho v City and Hackney Health Authority* [1998]; see also Taylor, 2013). This development gives a clear mandate to organisations and individual professionals to invest in the development of social work knowledge based on sound research.

This book is written in an awareness of the range of sources of knowledge on which social workers and other professionals must draw in their practice (Pawson et al., 2003), including law, regulation, guidance, policy, procedure, standards, principles and contextual information about the client and family, their perspectives and community. The focus in this book is on one specific and very important aspect of knowledge for professional practice: the understanding and use of research. This may be research on 'what works', but it may also be research on perspectives of those using services, perspectives of those providing services, prevalence and incidence of psychosocial problems and issues, and understandings of care processes that inform a better service. As strategies for social work research and evidence-based practice develop (e.g. Health and Social Care Board, 2015) the need for a clearer understanding of key issues becomes pressing. Our aim is that this book will contribute to greater understanding and use of knowledge to inform all dimensions of professional social work practice. This is not necessarily straightforward, but is a challenge that must be faced if we are to thrive as a profession and provide the best service to clients, families and communities.

A commitment to 'public and patient' (user) involvement underpins our research and reviews of research (Boote et al., 2011; Hanley et al., 2004; E. Smith et al., 2009). With our post-qualifying, postgraduate students (social workers who are undertaking work-based projects with the support of their line management) we encourage them to involve a service user to advise on, for example, questionnaire design, and to invite clients who are respondents to participate in dissemination (Hanley et al., 2004). With Ph.D. students we normally recommend including clients and carers as part of the Advisory Panel or Doctoral Committee for the study. For studies in research grants such endeavours can go further, such as engaging peer-researchers in gathering and analysing data (Taylor et al., 2014). Given the target audience, in this book we have integrated aspects of service user involvement within chapters organised according to the main stages of the work. The reader interested in exploring service user involvement further is referred to the extensive materials produced by INVOLVE (see Further Reading, below). We also bear in mind here that practitioners, policy makers and the general public are users of research who need to be enabled to understand research essentials to interpret it to their own context and decisions.

Outline of the book

The book begins with a general chapter (Chapter 2) on the nature of knowledge in social work. This paints the broader philosophical and professional context for our focus on understanding and using research, which is a primary source of knowledge for any profession that seeks to serve people and provide a quality service. Chapter 3 focuses on defining the practice question for which evidence from research might be useful. It is essential that the practice evidence question is defined clearly and appropriately if subsequent efforts are not to be wasted. The focus of Chapter 4 is on what is commonly regarded as the first stage of systematically reviewing the literature: the practicalities of identifying relevant research, primarily through the web-based bibliographic databases and web search engines that are now available. A template to assist with this is provided in Appendix 4.

The following three chapters deal in turn with appraising the quality of **surveys**, of qualitative studies and of studies of effectiveness, thus addressing what is commonly regarded as the second stage of a systematic review of research evidence. This division has been chosen to reflect the main different types of study question for which different designs are suited. Surveys (see Chapter 5) are best suited to measuring the **prevalence** of something within a **population** (a defined group of people) and to examine correlations between characteristics of that population. Most of the points in this chapter about survey methods apply equally to the extraction of **data** from files, whether paper or electronic. Chapter 5 also includes some introductory general material on the appraisal of research quality relevant to the subsequent two chapters. Qualitative methods (see Chapter 6) are best suited to exploring questions about why and how something happens from the perspective of people who have experienced that activity or process or phenomenon. Questions about the effects and effectiveness of a planned intervention (such as a social work intervention) are generally best answered by an **experimental** or **quasi-experimental** research design where this is possible.

These types of design, which address questions of the effects of interventions, are explained in Chapter 7. Study quality is not the same as quality of reporting.

Chapters 5, 6 and 7 have a common structure and link to a set of tools that have been provided in Appendices 1, 2 and 3 to assist in appraising surveys, qualitative and (quasi-)experimental research respectively. We gratefully acknowledge the Critical Appraisal Skills Programme (CASP, 1998), which has inspired our own development of appraisal tools. To facilitate ease of use and to encourage readers to engage with and understand a range of research methods, the tools have a common overall structure but the prompts within these headings are specific to the type of research design. The basic concepts – including validity – underpin quality and credibility in surveys, experiments and qualitative studies, but have to be applied differently in each case.

Appraisal tools ensure consistent consideration of key aspects of study quality. We are very aware of the danger of using appraisal tools if they convey the impression that one can simply add up scores so as to give a meaningful overall score of quality. Does strength in one aspect of the study make up for weakness in another aspect? In this book study quality is defined in relation to the widely accepted criteria, including design criteria for appraising studies of effectiveness. The appraisal tools in the Appendices embody a multidimensional approach to appraising quality-balancing consistency with relevance to the type of research question and the broader context of the study (Wells and Littell, 2009). As in social work practice, the tools are there to be used to inform professional judgement, not to be followed robotically as if the tool in itself will provide 'the answer' through some mystical process (Taylor, 2013).

There is an inherent challenge in writing this book – and for the profession itself – in helping all social workers to develop sufficient understanding of research in order to make good use of it, while not attempting to cover all the knowledge and skills necessary to carry out research, which is not necessary for every social worker. This tension is particularly acute in Chapters 5, 6 and 7; we look forward to readers' comments on how well we have struck the balance.

Chapter 8 considers how research is synthesised to produce a coherent message for practice, the third stage of systematic approaches to reviewing research. We consider **meta-analysis** as a method for statistical combination of quantitative **findings**, and **meta-synthesis** as a method for combining qualitative studies using qualitative methods, as well as narrative synthesis methods. Chapter 8 also includes an introduction to the work of the Cochrane and Campbell Collaborations in systematic reviewing of the best evidence of interventions relevant to social work. Chapter 9 then puts the endeavours of the previous chapters into the context of how this evidence will be used to inform social work decisions, both in terms of individual practice and within organisations.

The focus of this book is on understanding and using the most common research designs that will be of interest to social workers and professionals in allied fields in order to extend their **knowledge** and thus inform their practice. The reader interested in developing the knowledge and skills to carry out research is referred to Campbell et al. (2016). The sections on appraising research necessarily require a focus on research methods and some selection among the wide range of methods available. Our focus here is on the main methods of interest: surveys, qualitative research and (quasi-) experimental studies. Although the title of this book focuses on understanding and using **research**, the main messages in this book about identifying, appraising, synthesising and using evidence to inform practice apply also to **service evaluation** and **professional audit** projects as well as research. We do not attempt to teach all the detail of statistical methods.

A Glossary clarifies terms used in this book, which are indicated by **bold** at the first mention in the text.

Some social workers in the UK prefer the term 'service user' to 'client'. The best evidence available suggests that this terminology is not a preference of people who come to social workers for help (Covell et al., 2007; Keaney et al., 2004; Lloyd et al., 2001). It may be that the current vogue for the term 'service user' in the UK is driven by political ideology rather than by people who come into contact with social workers (Heffernan, 2006). One of the people skilled by experience who assists in teaching on our qualifying social work programme is adamant that he does not want to be called a 'service user', seeing the term as having many negative connotations. The traditional and international term 'client' seems to convey better the professional responsibility of the social worker for his or her actions (Seal, 2008, pix), which is a key principle underpinning this text about the use of best evidence to inform practice. The professional relationship, where the social worker contributes a particular area of knowledge and skills within an ethical framework, remains at the heart of effective social work practice. This is better conveyed by the term 'client' so this is often used here, although patient, survivor, tenant, recipient (of services), resident, day centre member, service user and customer may be used occasionally depending on the context.

In keeping with the interactive style of the SAGE/Learning Matters series, the text is interspersed with a number of features entitled Research Summary, Review Summary, Case Study, Activity and Becoming a Social Worker, as well as other illustrative material to prompt reflection and creative thinking. A range of helpful materials is listed as Further Reading at the end of each chapter. Where Further Reading is relevant to more than one chapter, it is included at the first relevant chapter. As mentioned above, this book includes, as appendices, tools that can be used to structure an appraisal of survey, qualitative and (quasi-)experimental research. These have been developed by the authors based on over a decade of teaching research methods and evidence-based practice to social workers on post-qualifying, postgraduate courses, doctoral students and student social workers on qualifying courses, as well as our own experimentation with appraisal of research (Taylor et al., 2007a). We hope you find them useful.

Further Reading

Campbell Collaboration (C2) www.campbellcollaboration.org

The Campbell Collaboration is an international, non-profit and independent organisation dedicated to making available up-to-date, accurate information on the effectiveness of social, behavioural, educational and criminal justice interventions. The Collaboration produces guidance on systematic reviewing of studies of effectiveness of interventions in criminal justice, education, social welfare (in its broadest sense) and international development using methods modelled on those of the Cochrane Collaboration.

Cochrane Collaboration (CC) www.cochrane.org

The Cochrane Collaboration is an international, non-profit and independent collaboration of about 30,000 people from over 100 countries dedicated to making up-to-date, accurate information about the effectiveness of health and social care interventions readily available. The Collaboration produces guidance on systematic reviewing of studies of effectiveness of interventions in health and social care. As well as a widely available online library, reviews are available in audio podcast form (www. cochranelibrary.com/more-resources/cochrane-podcasts.html).

INVOLVE www.invo.org.uk/

INVOLVE is funded by the National Institute for Health Research (NIHR) in the UK to promote public involvement in health and social care research. The organisation produces a wealth of valuable materials including on service user involvement in all stages of research. The evidence library has a database of about 300 references on this topic (www.invo.org.uk/resource-centre/evidence-library/).

Medical Research Council (2008) Developing and Evaluating Complex Interventions. London: MRC. Available at: www.mrc.ac.uk/documents/pdf/complex-interventions-guidance/

This Medical Research Council (MRC) document very helpfully outlines key stages in developing a complex intervention (such as most interventions by social workers), acknowledging the respective place of theory, and of qualitative and quantitative research according to the phase of development being addressed. It is a valuable framework for conceptualising the creation, development and evaluation of social work interventions.

National Institute for Health Research (2010) Systematic Reviews: Knowledge to support evidence-informed health and social care. London: NIHR. Available at: www.nihr.ac.uk/documents/about-NIHR/NIHR-Publications/NIHR-Systematic-Reviews-Infrastructure.pdf

This document outlines key stages and principles for robust reviews of evidence to support decisions about funding of health and social care interventions.

Rutter, D, Francis, J, Coren, E and Fisher, M (2010) SCIE Research Resource 1: SCIE systematic research reviews: Guidelines (2nd edition). London: Social Care Institute for Excellence. Available at: www.scie.org.uk/publications/researchresources/rr01.pdf

This is the Social Care Institute for Excellence guidance for systematic reviews of the effectiveness of social care (including professional social work) interventions in the UK. It is modelled on the guidance of the Cochrane and Campbell Collaborations but with a stronger dimension of involving clients and with standards for useful reviews that can be achieved with more limited resources than are used for CC and C2 reviews.

Chapter 2

What is knowledge and how does it inform practice?

Introduction

Central to social work's claim to be a profession is the premise that training provides an element of expertise relating to a specialised knowledge base. It is this knowledge that explains social problems, defines needs and informs key decisions. This chapter will outline the body of information that social work claims as its knowledge base. It will consider the relationship between theory and social work practice, and also analyse efforts to introduce a more evidence-based approach. In the complex contested world of social work, knowledge does not automatically fit with practice. The social worker is required to deliberate on their experience in the light of the available evidence. This chapter will describe the role of reflection and consider how this important aspect of the learning process can be supported.

Much has been written about social work's ambivalence towards theoretical knowledge. Some writers suggest that the profession has developed a knowledge base that it can call its own while others argue that practice is informed by a broader range of perspectives. In considering social work decision making it is useful to investigate the available knowledge base and to examine the relationship between knowledge and practice. The United Kingdom government's modernisation agenda (Department of Health, 1998) encouraged social work to base interventions on research evidence, ensuring effectiveness and efficiency. To support such evidence-based practice the United Kingdom government established the Social Care Institute for Excellence (SCIE) with the motto 'better knowledge for better practice' and the aim to:

> *Identify and spread knowledge about good practice to the large and diverse social care workforce and support the delivery of transformed, personalised social care services.*

(SCIE, 2008, www.scie.org.uk)

Social work practice is under increased scrutiny in courts and multidisciplinary settings and by the media; authority has less acceptance as a justification for interventions. As with other expert professionals, social workers are required to evidence that their actions are based upon a defensible conclusion (*Bolitho v City and Hackney Health Authority* [1998].

There is a growing acceptance that social workers need to find ways to evaluate the impact of practice on people who use the services. Initial efforts have highlighted the complexity of this process. However, in the last decade the debate has slowly moved from *why* social workers should use research evidence to *how* social workers should use research evidence.

Social work knowledge

Much of the knowledge that social work claims comes from communication studies, psychology, health and law. Trevithick (2008) identifies the three areas of (1) practice knowledge; (2) theoretical knowledge; and (3) factual knowledge that inform social work practice. The existence of a discrete knowledge base has been seen as an essential element of social work's claim to credibility, authority and professionalism. Jackie Pray outlined the importance of this quest for knowledge to ensure public confidence in social work: *Possession of knowledge – particularly scientifically derived knowledge – was thought to lead to reasonably accurate assessments and diagnosis, to effective treatment and to the ultimate alleviation of the client's misery* (Pray, 1991, p81).

Accuracy and effectiveness have long been priorities for the purchasers and planners of social services who wish to achieve value for money while avoiding negative outcomes. Healthcare is often presented as an example of a knowledge-based discipline to which others should aspire. Medical knowledge tends to be developed empirically in relation to clearly defined interventions and, as such, once established it can be readily applied to the appropriate case.

The social work knowledge base is neither unique nor universally accepted and a constructivist ethos means that there are few absolute truths. In the complex and uncertain social world, knowledge is context specific and meaning is relative to the perspectives of the various participants. Social workers often claim to use knowledge eclectically in response to the changing needs of their clients. While such a dynamic approach has some merit, it results in each worker picking and mixing their own personal understanding based on a large or small range of sources. This results in a nebulous relationship between knowledge and practice. Social worker interventions may be based on any of a number of models and methods. It is also possible that some interventions have no identifiable basis in theory or research whatsoever. Although the workforce continues to strive to improve the well-being of those in our care, the basis of social work practice cannot be methodically scrutinised and practice cannot be held to account.

Knowledge Example

Knowledge from a systematic review

The authors of this Campbell Collaboration review searched for, scrutinised, selected and synthesised 102 articles comparing kinship care with foster care in the areas of safety, permanency, and well-being of the child. While some methodological weaknesses were found in the studies, the authors conclude that kinship care is a viable option for children removed from home.

(Winokur et al., 2014)

Reading and not reading

It is generally assumed that social workers gain a repertoire of knowledge in their training that they apply and develop in their practice. However, an increasing body of research indicates that knowledge use within the profession is a much more complex issue.

Munro (2008) suggests that child protection social workers are inclined to rely on intuitive reasoning with limited analysis or application of theory. The limited **empirical** research relating to qualified social workers (Drury-Hudson, 1999; Fook, 2000; Osmond and O'Connor, 2006) suggests that formal (textbook) theory has little influence on social workers' conscious reasoning. Instead, these studies describe a skill-based approach where knowledge is related to processes (knowing how) or resources (knowing about). Social workers describe how their understanding of their role is based upon personal experience or discussion with others. This is summed up well by Barratt (2003) as *An oral rather than a knowledge-based culture within social work which results in staff valuing direct practice experience over, and often to the exclusion of, other forms of learning* (Barratt, 2003, p143).

The above research findings would seem to suggest that social work knowledge is gained through an apprenticeship or situated learning (Lave and Wenger, 1991) approach, where social workers are shown their trade in practice rather than being taught it in a classroom. Social workers' inability to verbalise their use of theory has led some to suggest that practitioners may have internalized the necessary knowledge to become unconsciously competent (Howell, 1982). Others (Sellick et al., 2002) have argued that social work should not seek to base its authority on formalised theory: *The true basis of our accountability lies in our willingness to expose our knowledge for what it is – our knowledge – and to invite engagement with it, dialogue* (p497).

Reflection, reflexivity and uncertainty

Reflection is the process by which social workers use knowledge to understand the issues and improve their practice. As Figure 2.1 shows, the reflection is part of the ongoing learning process where the practitioner develops knowledge and applies it to practice.

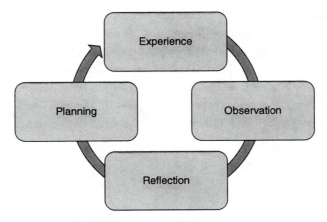

Figure 2.1   The learning cycle (adapted from Kolb and Fry, 1974)

Darragh and Taylor (2008) stress the importance of reflection in supporting the helping process, professional decision making and effective use of available resources. An IRISS study (Collins and Daly, 2011) interviewing practitioners found that reflection was seen as critical to the decision-making process. Supervision was often the setting where reflection took place, although opportunities were sometimes limited by time constraints.

Donald Schön's (1983) classic text on the reflective practitioner identified the challenges of the existing technical rational approach for many occupations including social work. Schön recognised that a rigorous approach to knowledge excluded the more subjective information that was vital to the social work role. His topographical metaphor clearly illustrates the dilemma:

> *There is a high, hard ground where practitioners can make effective use of research-based theory and technique, and there is a swampy lowland where situations are confusing messes incapable of technical solution. The difficulty is that the problems of the high ground, however great their technical interest, are often relatively unimportant to clients or the larger society, while in the swamp are the problems of the greatest human concern.*

(Schön, 1983, p42)

Schön described the artful use of common sense or knowledge-in-action to produce reflection-in-action or reflective conversation with the situation. An honest recognition of the strengths and weaknesses of this form of thinking on your feet can be positive for both the client and the practitioner. Importantly, in a subsequent book Schön (1987) suggested that practitioners could be taught to be reflective and therefore more effective in their decision making.

In the years since Schön's writing, efforts have been made to promote more explicit, effective decision making (e.g. Krysik and Finn, 2013) but the profession seems reluctant to submit itself to such scrutiny. Eileen Gambrill (2001) argued that social work could not show its interventions to be any more effective than those of non-professionals.

Gambrill described social work as an authority-based profession arrogantly using pseudoscience to justify its existence: *Bamboozling the public and those who fund service programs into believing that professionals offer unique services that require specialised training and experience* (Gambrill, 2001, p170). Gambrill argued that the move away from an authority-based profession required greater involvement of service users and a greater transparency of actions. Practitioners and service users should have access to sound research findings, and social work interventions should be open to rigorous **evaluation**.

Theoretical Summary

Reflective practice model

This model identifies five domains of social work practice and the following five-stage process where the practitioner can consider the relevance of each domain to specific casework.

Domains	Stages
Psychobiography	Reflecting on self
Relationship	Reflecting on the enabling process
Culture	Reflecting on the service user's experience
Organisation	Reflecting on social work practice
Politics/economy	Bringing it all together

(Houston, 2015)

Forms of knowledge

Writers from social work and other professions have sought to describe and categorise the range of information that is available to practitioners. The Social Care Institute for Excellence (SCIE, 2003) provided a valuable model for the classification of knowledge. This considered a range of available models and developed a model based on five possible sources of knowledge.

- **Organisational** – knowledge gained from organising social care.
- Practitioner – knowledge gained from doing social care.
- Policy community – knowledge gained from the wider policy context.
- Research – knowledge gathered systematically with a planned design.
- **User and carer** – knowledge gained from experience of and reflection on service use.

People who use services and those who care for them can assist in knowledge creation in three different ways. First, users and carers can assist in setting research priorities. Studies have shown that, if asked, service users can identify research themes and these are often different from those currently being pursued by practitioners and academics

(Thornicroft et al., 2002). Second, users and carers can contribute to the research activity as peer-researchers, particularly with hard to reach populations (Burns and Schubotz, 2009; Walsh and Boyle, 2009). Involvement can range from consultation to user-controlled research (INVOLVE, 2010). Finally, the perspective of those who use services is a valuable source of knowledge (Hoole and Morgan, 2011).

Distinguishing the potential sources of knowledge is helpful as it identifies the authority on which the material is based. Practitioners are able to use this information when analysing and applying the document. Practice decisions could benefit from the inclusion of a range of information sources allowing the triangulation of meaning. Each source provides a different perspective on the subject and, while they cannot be ranked in importance, it is important for practitioners to assess the credibility and relevance of each. To assist this process, SCIE presented six standards that would assist practitioners to judge the quality of knowledge from each of the identified sources. These formed the acronym TAPUPA.

- Transparency of the process of developing knowledge.

- Accuracy of all assertions.

- Purposivity – appropriate to the task in hand.

- Utility – fit for use.

- Propriety – legally and ethically produced.

- Accessibility – meeting the needs of potential users.

Tew et al. (2006) welcomed a quality measure that goes beyond scientific rigour to consider potential relevance, usefulness or emancipatory potential. However, SCIE stressed that the tool was a standards framework and as such it did not replace judgements about quality. The assessment of quality will be discussed later in this chapter and in the three appraisal chapters (5, 6 and 7) later in this book.

Knowledge Example

Service user knowledge

In this study, people with experience of mental health issues and the mental health care systems conducted focus groups to explore the role of psychiatric hospital care in promoting recovery. The findings show that the participants had a range of self-help techniques to promote recovery. On the hospital ward positive relationships with staff were seen as central to the patients' experience. A positive interaction between staff and inpatients usually left the patient feeling that they had been taken seriously and had been given adequate time to be heard. This usually resulted in raised levels of self-esteem, moving the patient a step closer towards recovery.

(Walsh and Boyle, 2009, p34)

Evidence-based practice

In the quest for measurable indicators of effective practice, policy makers and service planners embraced the concept of evidence-based practice (EBP). The policy and organisational dimensions of using research will be discussed in Chapter 9 of this book; the present chapter will focus on the use of EBP by the individual. This concept, which originated in medicine, was quickly adopted by other professions. Many writers (e.g. McKenna et al., 1999; Newman and McDaniel, 2005) attributed the genesis of the modern movement to Archie Cochrane's 1972 lecture and subsequent publication (Cochrane, 1972). Cochrane argued that ongoing resource limitations necessitated health and social care services to provide effectiveness, efficiency and equality:

> *If we are ever going to get the optimum results from our national expenditure on the NHS we must finally be able to express the results in the form of benefit and the cost to the population of a particular type of activity, and the increased benefit that could be obtained if more money were to be made available. For many reasons I do not think such an approach is possible, even on a narrow front, at present but I wanted to aim in the right direction.*

> (1972, p1)

Cochrane promoted the use of **randomised controlled trials** that would distil the findings from the best research, highlighting the key messages for practitioners. Cochrane's work in the UK was mirrored by Gene V. Glass in America, who coined the term 'meta-analysis' for an approach to the **synthesis** of quantitative data. Meta-analysis and other approaches to synthesising research are discussed further in Chapter 8 of this book. Twenty-five years later, Glass (2000) admits that his motivation in developing this scientific approach was reactive rather than considered. Not least among his objectives was his *wish to annihilate Eysenck and prove that psychotherapy really works, and my need to make a big splash with my Presidential Address* (Glass, 2000, Internet reference):

Defining evidence-based practice

While there is a range of differing definitions of evidence-based practice, many writers use that proposed by David L. Sackett et al. in a *British Medical Journal* (BMJ) editorial:

> *Evidence-based [practice] is the conscientious, explicit and judicious use of current best evidence in making decisions about the care of individual patients. The practice of evidence-based medicine means integrating individual clinical expertise with the best available external clinical evidence from systematic research.*

> (1996, p71)

The struggle to define evidence-based medicine was mirrored in the field of social care. The discipline was initially embraced by writers who wished to see more explicit and scientific approaches to the social work process (e.g. Gambrill, 1999;

Gibbs, 1991; Macdonald, 2000; Sheldon and Macdonald, 1999). Sheldon and Macdonald (1999) described practitioners' lack of empirical knowledge, and they attributed this to inadequate professional training, organisational obstacles and limited availability of quality research **evidence**. The theme was developed by Eileen Gambrill (2001) who argued that without rigorous evaluation, social work was unable to justify the interventions that it uses. She suggested that to date social work had been based on authority and good intentions rather than proven outcomes. Gambrill highlights the dichotomy between this approach and social work ethics: *I see a deep thread of insincerity in our profession. Many are insincere in their efforts to help clients, if by* **sincere**, *we mean caring enough to draw on practice-related research findings, carefully evaluate the effects of services, and involve clients as involved participants* (Gambrill, 2001, p172). Gibbs (2003) has provided a redefinition of evidence-based practice using a values perspective that urges the practitioner to continually seek the evidence that will allow them to best meet the needs of the people who receive their service: *Placing the client's benefits first, evidence-based practitioners adopt a process of lifelong learning that involves continually posing specific questions of direct practical importance to clients, searching objectively and efficiently for the current best evidence relative to each question, and taking appropriate action guided by evidence* (Gibbs, 2003, p6).

The importance of EBP

Much of the early material supporting an evidence-based approach to social work (e.g. Macdonald et al., 1992 in the UK; Gambrill, 2001 in the USA) stressed the need to establish the effectiveness of social work rather than *to present good intentions as evidence of good outcomes* (Gambrill, 2001) as the concept of evidence-based practice took shape to promote understanding and activity.

The value of an evidence-based approach to social work and social care has been considered in relation to agencies, practitioners and service users. In an SCIE report, Marsh and Fisher (2005) highlight six reasons for an evidence-based approach to social care:

1. the impact of professional decisions on people's immediate circumstances;

2. the impact of professional decisions on people's futures;

3. the need to challenge fundamental assumptions;

4. the need for safeguards where professionals have extensive powers;

5. informing the public; and

6. informing service users and enabling them to participate in decision making.

Other writers echo these themes of quality (what's best?), efficacy (what works?) and equality (who decides?) linking them to core social work values. However, they seem less enthusiastic than their medical counterparts to consider the theme of value (how much?).

Barriers to evidence-based practice

Academics continue to debate the nature of evidence but different barriers to evidence-based practice exist in the workplace. Health and social care practitioners have been shown to be unable or unwilling to apply research findings to their practice (Sheldon and Macdonald, 1999; Sinclair and Jacobs, 1994; Tozer and Ray, 1999). This deficiency is similar in other professional groups and recent studies have sought to identify the causal factors. Stevens et al. highlighted the poor fit between the available research findings and the needs of social care staff. When seeking sound evidence to support social care practitioners, Stevens et al. found the following:

> Most interventions of interest had not been soundly evaluated. If the research base is patchy, there is a danger of over-prioritising interventions that have been well evaluated while others that have not been evaluated may at least be as effective or more so.

(2005, p73)

Shlonsky and Gibbs (2006) argue that practitioners can be taught the skills to search for and appraise relevant research evidence. This can be supported by systematic reviews that select quality studies relating to a topic and synthesise the meaning in a way that is accessible to the practitioner (Shlonsky et al., 2011b). Shlonsky encourages the use of Cochrane Collaboration and Campbell Collaboration databases of systematic reviews. He also suggests that the task of searching can be quicker and more effective if the practitioner understands the effective use of filters and journals use standardised key words (Shlonsky et al., 2011a).

Messages from healthcare

Using an information economics perspective, Coiera (2001) provided a valuable summary of the potential costs and benefits of evidence-based guidelines to practitioners, clients and agencies. Coiera accepted that EBP had significant cost implications for the practitioner, and he suggested that many of the benefits were experienced by the client or agency. In many cases the costs faced by the clinician involved time and those faced by the healthcare system involved resources. For both, such costs are emphasised by the time and financial pressures that they already face. Coiera encouraged the medical community to reduce the potential costs while increasing the benefits to all parties:

> Optimistically, the economic way of thinking will result in the creation of a true evidence marketplace. Here, those who choose the evidence, whether patient or clinician, interact with those who create it to produce the optimum outcome for the community as a whole, harnessing its natural competition and selection forces to evolve our notions of evidence-based practice.

(2001, p670)

Promoting research-minded practice

The large body of knowledge relating to evidence-based practice and its implementation has been systematically reviewed by a number of writers and groups. The Cochrane Review Group on Effective Practice and Organisation of Care (EPOC) undertakes: *Systematic reviews of educational, behavioural, financial, regulatory and organisational interventions designed to improve health professional practice and the organisation of health care services, potentially spanning any clinical area* (EPOC, 2008, www.epoc. cochrane.org).

In 1999, EPOC collaborated with the University of York's NHS Centre for Reviews and Dissemination (CRD) (Wilson et al., 2001) in publishing a summary of systematic reviews of interventions to promote research utilisation among medical staff. The study found that dissemination alone had limited impact, while well-resourced, multifaceted approaches targeted to an identified need were most effective. In an SCIE publication, Walter et al. (2004) developed the CRD analysis to provide seven forms of research promotion.

- *Ensuring a relevant research base.* Partnerships like Making Research Count (Humphries, 2003) have been developed between researchers and practitioners in identifying and commissioning research activity.

- *Ensuring access to research.* The Cochrane and Campbell Collaborations seek to review high quality and up-to-date evidence for use by health and social care staff. Within social care, CEBSS and RIP (Barratt, 2003) are seeking to make relevant research findings available to staff.

- *Making research comprehensible.* Projects like *What Works for Children* (www. whatworksforchildren.org.uk/; Stevens et al., 2005) seek to provide research material in an understandable format.

- *Drawing out the practice implications of research.* SCIE produces practice guides and SCARE briefings that synthesise the most relevant research on specific social care topics.

- *Developing best practice models.* Organisations including the electronic Library for Social Care (eLSC) and the Joseph Rowntree Fund seek to produce and disseminate guides to best practice.

- *Requiring research-informed practice.* Social care services are facing increased pressure from external bodies to provide a research basis for the work. Some agencies are taking a proactive role in encouraging evidence-based practice from within.

- *Developing a culture that supports research use.* Some organisations have made specific efforts to promote a culture of research mindedness. Barnardo's (Newman and McDaniel, 2005; Newman and McNeish, 2002) has sought to use research to inform practice and to use evaluation to develop the existing knowledge base.

(Walter et al., 2004, pp13–23)

Walter et al. recognised the complexity of the research utilisation process and throughout the document they used the term 'research-informed practice' as a more realistic aspiration than researched-based practice or evidence-based practice.

Models of research utilisation

The utilisation of research findings by policy makers and practitioners has been extensively studied. The simplistic concept of a linear relationship has been widely criticised (e.g. Stevens et al., 2005) as has the enlightenment model (Weiss, 1979) that presumed that findings will eventually be absorbed into practice. Similar criticism has been levelled at the political model (Weiss, 1979) where direct links are subjectively made to support a pre-existing ideology or argument. Politicians and policy makers tend to be selective in their use and interpretation of research evidence. Some commentators have asked whether we are pursuing evidence-based policy or policy-based evidence (Marmot, 2004).

Speaking at a meeting in 2003 of the Overseas Development Institute (Britain's leading independent think tank on international development and humanitarian issues), Vincent Cable, then MP for Twickenham, provided a candid view of the way that politicians extract and process information from research:

> I thought that one way of differentiating between the way that someone like me operates and the way that researchers operate is in terms of a series of 's's which seem to summarise the political world quite well: speed, superficiality, spin, secrecy and scientific ignorance.

(Cable, 2004)

Walter et al. (2004) identify three modes of research use that apply to social care. The research-based practitioner model requires each staff member to source and assimilate the knowledge required to inform good practice. This model presumes that practitioners are autonomous with control over their working environment. The model's primary weakness is its inability to incorporate the major organisational factors discussed earlier in this chapter. In the embedded research model, research findings influence practice indirectly through policy or practice guidelines. This model would seem to address many of the barriers to utilisation faced by practitioners as agencies and government departments take responsibility for the identification and application of research evidence. Pinkerton (1998) analysed the relationship between research and policy, and provided examples of important policies that are directly influenced by research. Interestingly, Pinkerton showed that the most influential research was not always the most rigorous. Walter et al. (2004) found that examples of research-informed policy were rare and many of the barriers to utilisation applied equally to policy documents. They expressed concern that the embedded research model might detract from the practitioners' sense of ownership, which is central to utilisation.

In Walter et al.'s (2004) third and final organisational excellence model, research utilisation is promoted by leaders within organisations. Such an organisational approach is supported by literature that particularly relates to the perceptions of practitioners. While there is some evidence that research training and partnerships have proved beneficial, this model has been criticised as an unrealistic aspiration. Walter et al. (2004) reference a small study by Hodson (2003) that identified a range of barriers that prevent leaders from promoting research at an organisational level.

Walter et al. (2004) identify strengths in each of the above models. They propose a whole system approach that incorporates these strengths to maximise the impact of quality research in social work and social care. Walter et al. identify six key stakeholders that have a role in supporting research utilisation:

1. governance and related organisations;

2. research funders, research organisations and researchers;

3. practice organisations, practice managers and practitioners;

4. training organisations and trainers;

5. service user organisations and service users;

6. facilitating organisations.

(2004, p45)

They suggest that the actions of all of these stakeholders need to be coordinated in a multifaceted and flexible approach that will address the needs of social care's diverse and complex roles.

Knowledge Example

Effective supervision

SCIE has produced a number of research briefings that summarise the key evidence in relation to a specific theme. In 18 pages the research briefing on *Effective Supervision in Social Work and Social Care* covers the following subjects.

- What is the issue?
- Why is it important?

(Continued)

(Continued)

- What do we know already?
- What this research briefing adds.
- What does the research show (including models and outcomes)?
- Implications for policy, practitioners, organisations, users and researchers.

The briefing finishes with a range of useful Internet resources.

(Carpenter et al., 2012)

Soydan and Palinkas (2014) provide guidelines for supporting a culture of evidence-based practice within the social work profession. This includes:

- a recognition of the diversity of the available knowledge base and an understanding of the contribution that each form makes to practice;

- an organisation where the leadership promotes innovation and learning;

- a formal infrastructure to support research activity and awareness; and

- strong links between practitioners and academics.

The social work profession places much credence on its ability to identify relevant knowledge and apply it in a manner that benefits people who use the service. It is generally assumed that a comprehensive knowledge base assists the practitioner in recognising and responding to social issues. Social work students are taught and examined on a range of theory as well as skills and values. Practice placements are central elements of social work training where students have the opportunity to link their book learning to practice settings. After qualifying, social workers have the opportunity to consolidate and then develop their use of knowledge in their specific setting. However, the complexity of the social world often defies categorisation and practitioners often describe a lack of fit between their casework and the available methods and models. This difficulty in utilising knowledge is emphasised as the profession seeks to engage in a more scientific process. In the ongoing debates among academics, the principle of a more evidence-based approach is generally accepted by social work managers and planners. In practice, however, the utilisation of research findings has proved to be a complex task. Those investigating the relationship between research and practice (e.g. Kitson et al., 1998; Walter et al., 2004) have raised interesting questions but more research is required to establish how best health and social care practitioners can reap the benefits envisaged by Archie Cochrane almost 25 years ago. This book is one step along a journey.

Becoming a social worker

It is important that a social worker is able to appraise research evidence provided from survey methods, whether they seek to describe the characteristics of a group or investigate the relationship between two or more variables.

Reflection Point

What knowledge is available to inform your practice and what additional material would be of benefit?

Activity 2.1

Evidence into practice task

- For your particular area of interest undertake a search for current material in each of the following categories.

  o Organisational – knowledge gained from organising social care.
  o Practitioner – knowledge gained from doing social care.
  o Policy community – knowledge gained from the wider policy context.
  o Research – knowledge gathered systematically with a planned design.
  o User and carer – knowledge from experience of and reflection on service use.

Chapter Summary

- Social work has a diverse knowledge base that includes organisational, practitioner, policy, research, and user and carer knowledge.
- Social workers use reflection to apply this range of information to their own practice setting.
- Evidence-based practice involves searching for the current best evidence relating to your client's needs and using this to inform interventions.
- There is a need for us to evaluate our interventions to establish how effective they are.
- Organisations can promote evidence-based practice with formal supports and a culture of learning and enquiry.

Further Reading

Fischer, J (2009) *Toward Evidence-Based Practice: Variations on a theme.* Chicago, IL: Lyceum.

The reader interested in the evolution of ideas, principles and skills for evidence-based practice is referred to this monumental work that brings together papers by the author written over four decades.

Gibbs, LE (2003) *Evidence-Based Practice for the Helping Professions: A practical guide with integrated multimedia.* Pacific Grove, CA: Brooks/Cole.

This book lays out a comprehensive framework for evidence-based practice focusing on social work, although it is designed for all human-service professions.

Macdonald, G and Popay, J (2010) Evidence and practice: The knowledge challenge for social work in Shaw, I, Briar-Lawson, K, Orme, J and Ruckdeschel, R (eds) *The SAGE Handbook of Social Work Research.* London: SAGE, 264–80.

In this erudite chapter Geraldine Macdonald and Jennie Popay lay out the challenge for social work in developing a profession that makes use of evidence in practice.

Chapter 3

Practice questions and research types

Introduction

This chapter focuses on the topic of asking a clear question to inform the construction of a search on bibliographic databases or on the Internet for relevant research that addresses the question. Sometimes people do not state clearly what they really wanted to know, or do not phrase their question precisely enough for it to be answerable. This is very important when searching for research to inform practice. The question must be framed in a way that could be addressed by an appropriately designed research, evaluation or **audit** study, and such that the search can be translated into some sort of **search formula** to use on a bibliographic database or an Internet search engine to identify relevant studies.

In this chapter we outline key types of questions and identify types of research that are most likely to be used to address these types of question. Our focus is on questions about:

- experiences of problems, receiving or providing services (addressed primarily by **qualitative research**);
- questions of prevalence and correlation (e.g. of social needs, addressed primarily by **surveys**); and
- questions about the effectiveness of services (addressed primarily by **experimental** or **quasi-experimental studies**).

The chapter considers, but in less detail, questions of incidence of referrals and events, about predictive factors and about the causes of problems. We also discuss types of questions addressed by service evaluation and professional audit, including the accessibility and suitability of services. The chapter concludes with sections on client aspects of defining the question, defining the scope of the question in terms of time and place, and frameworks for structuring practice evidence questions.

Types of questions

Specifying a precise question for a review of the literature is a similar task to specifying a precise question for a research project. How tightly you define the topic may depend on how much published literature there is in the field. You want to create a manageable process within your time and resources and must manage the breadth of the topic as an aspect of that. Asking the correct question is important because the primary issue in appraising the appropriateness of the design of a study is the type of question being asked rather than the topic under consideration. Almost any research design can be used in any topic area, subject to practicalities and ethical issues. The main issue is the type of question being asked about the topic.

A profession is defined by its focus on providing a service to people rather than merely studying them as a purely academic discipline does. This is true of social work. It is important that questions you pose yourself for reviewing research are related in some way to the services that we provide for people as social workers. One way to do this is to locate your question in relation to the very helpful Medical Research Council framework for developing and evaluating complex interventions (2008). The way that the framework is described makes it very useful for social care as well as for healthcare – most social work could be described as complex in this context. We often have to deal with systems of people (including families) rather than individuals themselves. Even where we deal with individuals, we are normally addressing diverse aspects of their lives within society (including family, neighbour and work roles), and various aspects of their emotional and social functioning. These multiple dimensions make our social work interventions complex.

In this context, the overarching paradigm for this book is that various types of research are required to address the different questions that are important at different stages of the process of creating and evaluating social work interventions. For example, a social need might be highlighted by a survey (gathering data on the prevalence and characteristics of problems). A theoretical formulation as to why some types of intervention might possibly be useful may be the next priority. The process of developing a useful intervention may then move on to explore the perceptions of those with problems, and recipients and providers of related services (probably using qualitative research) to inform the design of the intervention. Once we have an intervention designed in some preliminary form, some piloting is required to ensure that we have assessment tools that could measure change if the new intervention were successful. Then we would want to carry out some robust experimental or quasi-experimental study to measure the effect (if any) of the new intervention. Thus, diverse empirical and theoretical contributions are required in order to develop effective services (Medical Research Council, 2008). In a broader frame of reference, we could regard **inductive research** (typically qualitative) and **deductive research** (typically experiments or surveys) as complementary parts of the process of creating knowledge. To create knowledge that will enable us to develop effective social work interventions requires a range of types of research, each suited to addressing particular types of question.

It may be appropriate to shape the review of research to have a range of questions. For example, if the main question were about the effectiveness of a particular intervention there may still be important questions about why it worked or did not work in various contexts and how the intervention was implemented or delivered in various contexts and countries. In social work we often want to know about the processes of delivering care or some intervention – and the mechanisms that lead to it being more or less effective – as well as measures of whether the intervention can be shown to have some effect with particular human problems. There is a decision to be made about the focus of the review of research in terms of the breadth of the question or group of questions, always keeping in mind that it must be a manageable and achievable process.

Questions about experiences of problems, and receiving or providing services

One question of interest to social workers delivering services is the perspectives of people on a particular experience. In our context, this may be the views of clients or families on the problems or the services that they have experienced, or it may be the views of providers of services on some aspect of the process of providing a service. Service providers would include foster parents, home-care workers, residential and day-care staff as well as professional social workers. As we understand such perspectives more deeply, we can create a construct, concept, paradigm or model to describe the 'world' from the perspective of these participants. This is the realm of qualitative research designs (see Chapter 6).

Client perceptions can usefully inform *how* we provide services, and qualitative methods are a useful tool for understanding 'their world'. Client conceptualisations of needs can provide an understanding of the problems that these types of clients face. Similarly, the perceptions of people providing services can lead to a conceptualisation of the dynamic of the helping process. This might provide useful insight into *how* services are most helpfully provided, as well as assisting in training novices to the work. Questions about the perceptions and conceptualisations of people about a personal experience, such as a psycho-social need or the receipt or provision of a personal service, are generally addressed most appropriately using a qualitative approach, particularly if the topic has emotional content or if we wish to 'understand their world'. Qualitative methods are discussed in Chapter 6.

Questions of prevalence and correlation

If we wish to know how common a particular problem is within a particular population (e.g. the prevalence of children having autism in relation to the total number of children), then we will be asking a question most commonly answered by survey research (see Chapter 5). Surveys can answer questions of this type by taking a **sample** of the population in question and inferring from this to the whole population of interest. These are also referred to as '**cross-sectional surveys**' to distinguish them from 'longitudinal surveys' which measure some variables at two or more points in time. The following are some examples of prevalence questions often appropriately addressed by surveys.

- What percentage of people with dementia are living alone in locality X?

- What fraction of social workers discuss risk issues with clients at the point of hospital discharge?

- What proportion of prisoners were abused as children?

- What fraction of children in state care have diagnosed mental health problems?

Surveys (with appropriate **sampling**) are generally most appropriate for measuring the prevalence of a variety of variables, not only client problems. Surveys might be used to measure the prevalence of aspects of people such as:

- attributes (what people *are*) – e.g. age, sex, marital status, income, offspring;

- behaviour (current);

- events (in the past);

- knowledge (of facts);

- beliefs (what people believe to be true);

- attitudes, opinions (value judgements);

- reasons for doing things.

Surveys are also well suited to comparing how the prevalence of something in a population compares with the prevalence of another factor – for example, we might want to ask the following types of question.

- How does the prevalence of the children in state care with diagnosed mental health problems compare with the prevalence of diagnosed mental health problems among children of similar age in the general population?

- How do emotional intelligence scores of social workers compare with those of profession X?

Surveys can be used effectively to explore correlations between factors such as in these questions. That is to say, we may be interested to know whether one problem occurs more often than one would expect by chance alongside another problem – for example, we might be interested to know that drug addiction problems correlate with suicidal ideation among teenagers receiving social work support. Or we may be interested to know whether something that we regard as a 'causal factor' correlates with a particular problem. For example, does being sexually abused in childhood correlate with mental health problems in adulthood (Davidson et al., 2010)? In this context, surveys are measuring the correlation of two (or more) variables in which we are interested.

Research Summary

Survey of prevalence and correlation

Self-harming and suicide amongst adolescents are reported to be increasing in Europe and internationally. For young people in state care this aspect of mental wellbeing is of particular concern. The aim of this study was to establish the incidence of suicidal ideation and behaviour amongst young people (age 16 to 21 years) leaving state care in one Health and Social Care Trust, and to explore the correlation between this and client risk factors that might inform professional practice. Data was gathered from 164 case files of the total 215 (response rate 76%) in relation to all open cases at 30 April 2012 extracted by the relevant Social Workers through the use of a standard data collection tool. Twenty-seven per cent of young people known to the 16+ Teams engaged in self-harm or suicidal behaviour. There was a strong correlation between the number of self-harm incidents and the number of suicide attempts. The risk factors identified were consistent with the research base: 'male', 'unemployed', 'alcohol and drug misuse', 'adverse childhood experiences', 'higher number of placement moves', 'placement type' and 'older age when entering care'. Young people in more isolated placements seemed particularly at risk. The results of this study are of particular relevance to Social Workers and other professionals working with young people leaving state care.

(Hamilton et al., 2015)

Service evaluations and professional audit projects generally include a survey component. They might include questions about the length of time clients spend in assessment processes, or the satisfaction scores of service recipients with the service received.

Questions about the incidence of referrals and events

A related type of question to those of prevalence is that we may wish to know how often some event occurs – for example, the **incidence** of falls among residents in nursing homes during the first week after admission or the incidence of violence in children's homes during each month of the year. Such incidence questions are suited to a survey design, often using **secondary data** sources such as records of services. The key dimension where a measure of incidence is different from a measure of prevalence is that a time period needs to be specified. Various dimensions need to be considered in defining the time period, such as being as recent as possible if we want an up-to-date review, and creating a manageable data set.

Questions about predictive factors

Surveys of prevalence as outlined above can provide information on whether factors correlate with each other, but are weak evidence in showing that one factor causes another one. For example, a survey finding that addiction problems and mental health problems correlate among teenagers in state care does not tell us which of these causes the other or whether there is some independent, unknown cause of both. A design that is stronger for this purpose is a **case-control study**, which identifies two groups from among a group of people. For example, this might be those ending up with the particular problem and those who do not, or those who have a 'successful' outcome from social work intervention and those who do not. The characteristics of the two groups are then compared to identify factors that are significantly different.

Case Example

Designing a case-control study

A case-control study might be used to identify factors that predict the successful return home of people discharged from psychiatric hospital.

1. Use a large and representative data set on people discharged from psychiatric hospital.
2. Define information in the records that distinguishes successful from unsuccessful return home.
3. Divide the data into two groups: those regarded as successful and those regarded as unsuccessful in return home.
4. Enter the characteristics of the individuals, their problems and their home circumstances, etc. into a multivariate analysis to identify factors that correlate with (un)successful return home.

Case-control studies have to date had limited use in social work, and thus we give them limited attention here. The interested reader is referred to Thyer (2010) in the Further Reading section or to Rubin and Bellamy (2012) for more extensive coverage.

Questions about the effectiveness of services

One type of question of interest, but not necessarily easy to answer, is whether an intervention has a measurable effect in reducing some problem for an individual or family. As a profession that seeks to help people to change (to overcome problems or to improve or maintain some aspect of quality of life), important questions we need to ask are about the effectiveness of our social care (including social work) interventions. Having some understanding of what is an appropriate intervention for a presenting client need is central to social work. If our interventions are not effective, we are wasting our clients' and our own time and energy, and deluding society and ourselves. Some examples of questions of effectiveness are illustrated below.

- Is family group conferencing effective in preventing reoffending by offenders under 15 years of age?

- Which type of counselling approach is more effective in mild depression: cognitive behavioural therapy or solution-focused brief therapy?

Questions about the effects (effectiveness) of planned interventions are addressed most robustly using some form of experimental or quasi-experimental study. In essence, an experimental study is where some people are randomly allocated to receive the service of interest and another similar group of people (equally randomly allocated) does not receive this service. The two groups are then compared in terms of outcomes. The detail of what constitutes an experimental study is discussed in Chapter 7 and these items also have an entry in the Glossary and in Taylor (2012a). There is a range of study designs that might address a question about effectiveness of services, and in this book we are taking a broad approach and referring to these as 'quasi-experimental'. Examples of experimental and quasi-experimental studies are given in Chapter 7.

Service evaluation and professional audit

If you are faced with the task of 'evaluating a service', you may wish to gather some quantitative data and some qualitative data. For example, we might want numeric data on how many people use the service and for how long, and the profile of clients in terms of needs or geographic location. We might also want some verbal (qualitative) data from clients expressing their perception on receiving the service, and from providers on the strengths and limitations of the service from their perspective. This is a simultaneous mixed-methods design. There are also mixed-methods designs that use qualitative data to inform the design of a survey or an experiment, or which use a qualitative study after a survey or experiment to better understand the **results**. Note that a thorough evaluation of a service in terms of its effects in achieving the planned change in the lives of clients would need a consideration of the issues discussed in relation to questions of effectiveness (see above and Chapter 7).

Research Summary

Mixed-methods service evaluation

Background: *Young people with disabilities are often excluded from the labour market. This paper describes a qualitative evaluation of an innovative two-year pilot initiative (VOTE) aiming to provide employment, training and support for vulnerable young adults with a wide range of disabilities.*

Aims: *The principal aims of the study were to assess the impact of the new service in the extent to which it had (1) created and developed training and employment opportunities for young people; and (2) promoted inclusive working partnerships.*

Method: *Documentary analysis was used as a basis for describing and assessing the project objectives in combination with face-to-face interviews with a small number of key stakeholders.*

Results: *A total of 122 young people participated in the initiative in the pilot period, during which time 160 vocational qualifications were obtained. Key stakeholders expressed positive views about the initiative and, in particular, its therapeutic benefits and the extent of inter-agency working and shared learning. The engagement with local employers was a noteworthy feature of the initiative in some localities.*

Conclusion: *The VOTE initiative achieved considerable success in empowering a significant proportion of young adults to engage in society by developing social and employment skills, and by improving their employment opportunities and prospects. Factors critical to the continued success of this and similar initiatives include: the matching of employment and training opportunities to client needs, abilities and aspirations; addressing the concerns of local employers; and the sympathetic treatment of workplace issues.*

(Taylor et al., 2004)

Questions about accessibility and suitability of services might be addressed by qualitative or survey research. If we know relatively little about this topic, then qualitative research would be appropriate to help us understand the concepts being used by the users of the service regarding what makes a service 'accessible'. If we already know key constructs – for example, the main public transport provision and its costs – then we could create survey questions to measure the prevalence of those issues among the service users.

Questions about the causes of problems

Perhaps the hardest questions to answer are those about the causes of social problems. An example would be whether exposure to violence on television causes aggressiveness, or the type and extent of harmful effects on children when parents separate.

Thankfully, except in some extreme regimes, societies generally do not allow experiments in which people are deliberately subjected to experiences that might cause them harm simply to observe the effect. However, **natural experiments** sometimes occur (such as when two groups of otherwise similar people undergo different experiences through no decision of the researcher), which can be used to good effect to study such factors (see examples in Medical Research Council, 2010). The features of experimental and quasi-experimental studies will be discussed further in Chapter 7.

More commonly, **longitudinal studies** are commonly used where individuals are followed over a lengthy time period to measure changes which might then be attributed to changes in their life circumstances. Longitudinal studies are an aspect of research where Great Britain is particularly strong as it is an island that has not been invaded for 1,000 years, and people generally have confidence in the government, so the records on individuals are of high quality. Without controls with which to compare, it is not easy to be confident as to the causes of the problems, but longitudinal studies are generally more robust than surveys in answering such questions. This area of research – the causes of social problems – might be termed 'social epidemiology' and is generally under-researched. There is limited involvement of social work in longitudinal research designs at the present time and the coverage in this book is therefore limited. The interested reader is referred to Engel and Schutt (2012).

Questions about a case example

Some papers that you read will report on a single 'case' of something. A case may be a person, group, team, organisation, community, country. In our context this might be:

- a single client – for example, relating to the problem or the change process or the outcome;

- the operation of a team, such as when it implements a new way of working;

- a case law judgment in its context and for its implications; or

- a study of a particular organisation or service, such as when it implements a new policy.

These types of papers are generally referred to as a '**case study**' or a **single subject design** or a 'single system design'. A case study can show the interconnection and complex nature of multiple dimensions of an issue. Such case studies are relatively easy to undertake but difficult to appraise in terms of quality, particularly as generalisability to other situations is rarely clear. There are some more complex studies occasionally called 'case studies' but which incorporate major components involving qualitative, survey or experimental research viewed as complementing each other. These are generally better considered in terms of the component parts in terms of appraising their quality even if the findings are viewed as cumulative in some way.

Questions on the quality of assessment tools

Some studies seek to study (and hence develop) the quality of assessment tools for professional (clinical) social work practice or for research purposes. Typically, such studies seek to appraise the validity, reliability or usability of the tools. **Validity** essentially means that the researcher is measuring what he or she claims to be – that is, the extent to which the design is a good test of the **hypothesis**. **Reliability** essentially means that a repeated use of the tool gives a similar result. Usability essentially refers to the ease of use of the tool. With the increasing use of validated assessment tools in social work (see e.g. Fisher and Corcoran, 2007a and 2007b) this is becoming an increasingly common area of research. While searching for studies relating to assessment tools is encompassed within this chapter, the reader interested in appraising assessment tools to measure client and family progress during interventions is referred to the excellent chapter in Rubin and Bellamy (2012).

Questions about decision making

There is increasing interest in studying decision making, or professional judgement, in social work. Research questions about decision making need to be framed carefully. Are we interested in the factors that influence a particular decision being made, or the processes by which an individual or a group reaches its decision? We need to clarify the extent to which a particular theoretical model is assumed in framing a question about decision making (Taylor, 2013). Questions about decision making may be addressed by all the major research designs considered in this book, for example:

- qualitative studies might seek to elucidate the conceptualisations that decision makers use in their cognitive decision-making process;

- surveys might be used to measure the factors that decision makers say influence their decisions or as part of a study of group processes in decision making; and

- experimental studies might be used to study the effects of an approach to improving decision making through some decision aid, or might be experiments of the type often posed by psychology laboratory studies presenting scenarios of some type for decision.

Client and public involvement in defining the question

Those who use services can bring a unique perspective to research questions in terms of the concepts and language that they use to describe their needs and their experience of services. The perspectives of clients on outcomes that are important or realistic may differ from the perspectives of those who provide services and those who manage them. The perspectives of people who use services are also valuable in ensuring that common-sense aspects of how interventions work are not ignored. The involvement of clients, families, users of research and other 'customers' of research in identifying research priorities is still in its infancy, but through organisations such as **INVOLVE** (see Further Reading in Chapter 1) the knowledge and skills to develop this are growing.

Clients and family carers can provide a valuable perspective on focusing the research question. For example, the mechanisms that facilitate or inhibit change are often under-researched, despite the efforts to shape interventions to meet needs. In a mixed-methods design of qualitative research followed by quantitative research, qualitative research with clients can inform the language used as well as the content of a subsequent survey.

Research Summary

Involving clients in research

This article seeks to contribute to the debate concerning the benefits and costs of involving young service users in research. The paper locates involvement within a continuum of consultation, collaboration and user-controlled research. The mandate for children and young people's involvement is identified. In particular, the paper focuses on the benefits and costs in relation to: research and development, research dissemination and service development, service users and researchers. The paper does not suggest that these benefits and costs can be measured arithmetically but argues that if the costs in terms of resources, training, support, timescale and remuneration are not addressed, the research will be undermined and in danger of becoming tokenistic. The article argues that the involvement of young service users as co-researchers is worthwhile, but that it should not be entered into lightly and that further work needs to be undertaken on which parts of the process young service users can be included in and where their involvement results in change in service delivery or service outcomes.

(McLaughlin, 2006)

There are various ways in which clients can inform research at various stages of the process. In general, these are beyond the scope of this book, and the interested reader is referred to the materials produced by the INVOLVE organisation as listed in the Further Reading section in Chapter 1.

Locating the question in time and place

If you are searching for research, evaluations or other materials to inform the development of your service, attention needs to be paid to issues of time and place or, if you prefer, 'geography and history'.

Considering place first, you need to consider how relevant studies will be to your situation if they are carried out in another country with different laws, culture and organisational arrangements. In general, questions that focus particularly on the biology or psychology of individuals, or on the relationships within families, are more likely to be generalisable across countries. By contrast, questions that relate to statutes, community and social culture or particular ways of organising services will require more 'translation' to derive their message for your own context. In general, it is unlikely that you will want to limit your search to papers that have been carried in or about your own geographical area even if it were readily possible on bibliographic databases or on the Internet.

Considering the time dimension, for most purposes you will want recent publications on your topic. However, it may be helpful to define how far back in time you wish to consider papers as 'relevant'. You might date your search from the time that some noteworthy relevant event occurred, such as:

- new legislation enacted;
- new policy introduced;
- new service delivery organisation commenced;
- introduction of a new way of working (e.g. family group conferencing); or
- a noteworthy social crisis in a country.

Frameworks for structuring questions

Various academics and professionals have created useful frameworks (usually with a readily memorable mnemonic) for structuring the key elements of a question about evidence to inform practice in health and human service occupations. The most widely known is the PICO framework, which is specific to questions of the effectiveness of an intervention. The acronym PICO stands for four key elements in defining a question about the effectiveness of an intervention.

- Population or Problem
- Intervention
- Comparator (Intervention)
- Outcome

(Centre for Reviews and Dissemination, 2009)

Population or problem

What is the population of people you are considering? What is the problem that these people face? What is the essential definition of their problem that you are seeking to address? Note that some generalisation is necessary in order to formulate a question that might be answered. You will need to consider the more individual characteristics of the client and family when you come to consider how to use the research knowledge to plan the way that the intervention is delivered.

Case Example

Defining the population or problem of interest

We might define the population or problem for the search as 'depression in adults'. The client may have strong views on the choice between counselling and medication as an intervention method. By contrast, the location of the counselling - for example, at home or at a clinic or office - is a question of process, not the essentials of the choice of intervention method which is the type of issue that we are trying to address with a question of effectiveness. In this case the age delineator 'in adults' is intended to exclude children and older people, in keeping with current theoretical understandings that these are better considered separately for the purpose of seeking to develop helpful interventions.

Intervention

What is the intervention that you wish to evaluate? How is this conceptualised and through what theory? How is the intervention conceptualised and defined in studies of its effectiveness? Are there variant forms of the intervention with different names? In order to ask questions about the effectiveness of an intervention you must be clear what is defined as being that intervention and what is not.

Case Example

Defining the intervention

The following terms were considered for a systematic review on 'Is Cognitive Behavioural Therapy effective for young offenders with substance abuse problems?' It was imperative that the intervention was defined consistently despite varying terminology.

Cognitive Therapy OR

Behaviour Therapy OR

Psychotherapy OR

Psychotherapy, Rational-Emotive OR

Cognitive behaviour therapy OR

CBT OR

aggression replacement training OR

moral reasoning OR

moral discussion groups OR

cognitive training OR

cognitive behaviour therapy OR

cognitive technique OR

cognitive therapy OR

cognitive restructuring OR

cognitive behavioural OR

dialectical behaviour therapy OR

social skills training.

(Campbell et al., 2010; the 'OR' operator between terms is explained in Chapter 4)

Comparator (intervention)

What is the comparator against which the intervention is to be compared? It may be that you wish to compare the intervention with 'usual treatment' or 'placebo' (no treatment). However, in some cases you may want to review the evidence that directly compares two different interventions.

Case Example

Defining the comparison intervention

We might wish to compare a computerised (online) version of an intervention with the face-to-face equivalent. For example, we might ask: 'How effective is computerised cognitive behavioural therapy compared to face-to-face cognitive behavioural therapy for adults with depression?' (see Olthuis et al., 2015).

Outcome

If you are asking a question about effectiveness, it is important to clarify a measurable outcome that is being sought as a result of the intervention. This is usually the outcome desired by the client, but might be something negotiated with family members (for example, within a family therapy intervention) or negotiated in relation to societal demands (for example, in relation to standards of child care and safeguarding). Authors of journal articles reporting studies of effectiveness will take care to include the main outcomes measures used in the abstract so as to facilitate retrieving the articles with a search on a bibliographic database. An outcome measure of interest might be the effectiveness of the intervention at preventing hospital admission, in which case our search question using the PICO structure might become 'How effective is computerised cognitive behavioural therapy compared to face-to-face cognitive behavioural therapy at preventing hospital admission for adults with depression?' An example of a search structure using PICO is given in Figure 3.1.

Review Question

Question: Is reminiscence therapy more effective than social contact for helping older people with dementia in daily behavioural functioning?

- Population: people over 65 years with dementia.
- Intervention: reminiscence therapy.
- Comparison intervention: social contact.
- Outcome measure: general behavioural functioning.

(see Woods et al., 2005)

P = Population (people) of interest

I = Intervention being studied

C = Comparator intervention being compared against

O = Outcome measure of interest

Figure 3.1 PICO structure for a search on the effectiveness of an intervention

Appropriate research designs for research questions

It is important to avoid the temptation to think of one research design or method as intrinsically better than any other, or that a particular topic in itself requires a particular method. The essential issue is the appropriateness of the research design and the data-gathering tools to the type of question that is being asked. Matching of questions to major research designs considered here is illustrated below.

- Client perspectives and processes of service delivery:
  - o strong: qualitative;
  - o weak: surveys.
- Effectiveness of an intervention:
  - o strong: experimental and quasi-experimental;
  - o weak: surveys and single-case design.
- Prevalence of problems in a population:
  - o strong: surveys.
- Factors predicting desirable and undesirable (harmful) outcomes:
  - o strong: surveys.
  - o weak: experimental and quasi-experimental.

(Adapted from Rubin and Bellamy, 2012, p63)

This structure of matching research types to question types is fully in accord with the framework of teaching on which this book is based.

Activity 3.1

Using the categories outlined above, identify the type of research question in the examples. What sort of research design might be most appropriate?

- What proportion of young people in state care have been physically abused?
- What is effective in helping sexually abused children to address mental health issues?
- What are the perceptions of older people on hospital discharge arrangements?
- What is the effect of a hospital discharge arrangement on likelihood of returning home?
- What is effective in reducing reoccurrence of crime by young adults?
- What are the signs and symptoms of drug addiction?
- How do older people conceptualise elder abuse?
- What is an effective way to prevent repeated self-harm amongst adolescents?
- How do adolescents who harm themselves perceive their behaviour?
- Why do some adolescents harm themselves?

Surveys (see Chapter 5) are best suited to measuring the prevalence of something within a population (a defined group of people) and to examining correlations between characteristics of that population. Qualitative methods (see Chapter 6) are best suited to exploring questions about why and how something happens from the perspective of people who have experienced that activity or process or phenomenon. Questions about the effects and effectiveness of a planned intervention (such as a social work intervention) are generally best answered by an experimental or quasi-experimental research design where this is possible. Where experimental designs are not possible, other designs such as case-control, longitudinal (cohort) and **interrupted time series (ITS) designs** may be used. These types of design are explained in more detail in Chapter 7.

Becoming a social worker

Being able to conceptualise questions related to their practice that are both useful and answerable is a key skill for a professional. This chapter relates particularly to domain 5.11 of the PCF on demonstrating an understanding of research methods, as an understanding of types of question is fundamental to understanding research methods as the quality of research can only be appraised in relation to the type of question it seeks to address.

Reflection Point

What types of questions would it be useful to have answers to in your practice?

Activity 3.2

Evidence into practice task

Create an effective question about an aspect of social practice with which you are familiar that is a question about one of the following.

- Client perspectives on processes of service delivery.
- Provider perspectives on processes of service delivery.
- Effectiveness of a social care (including social work) intervention.
- Prevalence of a particular problem in a population.
- Factors predicting desirable and undesirable (harmful) outcomes.

Identify an appropriate study design from the material in this chapter.

Chapter Summary

- To create knowledge that will enable us to develop effective social work interventions requires a range of types of research, each suited to its particular purpose.
- Inductive research (typically qualitative) and deductive research (typically experiments or surveys) are complementary parts of the process of creating knowledge.
- If you want to prove, measure, compare or contrast something you need a quantitative method.
- To explore experiences, perceptions and concepts in order to create a new theory or understanding, a qualitative method is likely to be most appropriate.
- Some type of survey design will be most appropriate if we wish to know about the prevalence or incidence of some behaviour, attitude or event, including for professional audit purposes.
- Some type of qualitative design will be most appropriate if we have a question about the perspectives or concepts of people – for example, on their needs or their experience of receiving or providing services.
- Some type of experimental or quasi-experimental design will be most appropriate if we have a question about the effect of a planned intervention.
- A simultaneous mixed-method design may be appropriate to give a rounded picture to evaluate a service or as part of a professional audit.

Further Reading

Cochrane Centre for the UK (2014) *Medical Literature Searching Skills: PICO: Formulate an answerable question.* Oxford: University of Oxford. Available at: http://learntech.physiol.hox.ac.uk/cochrane_tutorial/cochlibdoe84.php

This website provides a good summary (with visuals and examples) of the PICO structure for framing questions for a literature search on a question of the effectiveness of a health or social care intervention.

Gibbs, LE (2003) *Evidence-Based Practice for the Helping Professions: A practical guide with integrated multimedia.* Pacific Grove, CA: Brooks/Cole.

This book provides a sound reference point for ways of developing social work practice based on best evidence, including the COPES structure for framing questions for a literature search. Available at: www.evidence.brookscole.com/copse.html

Medical Research Council (2008) *Developing and Evaluating Complex Interventions.* London: MRC. Available at: www.mrc.ac.uk/documents/pdf/complex-interventions-guidance/

This document very helpfully outlines key stages in developing a complex intervention (such as most interventions by social workers are), acknowledging the respective place of theoretical, qualitative and quantitative research according to the phase of development being addressed. It is a valuable framework for conceptualising the creation, development and evaluation of social work interventions.

Thyer, BA (ed.) (2010) *The Handbook of Social Work Research Methods* (2nd edition). Thousand Oaks, CA: SAGE.

This is a valuable book providing a range of perspectives on research methods in social work, and how different methods address different types of questions.

Chapter 4

Identifying relevant research

Introduction

This chapter focuses on how to identify relevant research to use to inform practice. The place of peer-reviewed journal articles as the main mechanism for disseminating current research is explained. Major bibliographic databases relevant to social work are identified and their potential discussed. Effective and efficient ways to search these are explained and illustrated. We consider the potential and limitations of using the Internet to retrieve robust research and the use of 'grey literature'. Other methods of retrieving relevant research such as 'hand searching' and contacting authors are explained. The chapter concludes with a consideration of measuring the quality of a search and recording the search process. As with research methods itself, this is a topic where the various dimensions interplay with each other. We have tried to explain the aspects in a sequence that will be most readily understood, but inevitably there are still aspects where we signpost the reader to a more detailed explanation which comes later in the chapter.

Methods of identifying relevant research

Peer-reviewed journal articles

Regular publications, known as journals, have developed for each major area of human knowledge. It is in these journals that new research is published, although some journals will also publish material that is more theoretical, ideological or policy-oriented in nature. By comparison, textbooks usually present a synthesised range of established knowledge on a topic suited to a particular market of readers, rather than being the place to publish the findings of recent research. Journals are designed to publish up-to-date materials, including the primary presentation of findings of research. These academic journals typically publish a new issue between four and twelve times a year. The set of issues for a particular year is called a volume. As knowledge grows in innovative areas, new journals are created.

Each issue of a journal contains a number of articles, typically between five and twenty. For an article to be accepted for publication it must meet the requirements and standards of that journal, as decided by its Editorial Board. Normally, every manuscript submitted for consideration is sent to two peer reviewers familiar with the field for their comments. On some occasions there will be more than two reviewers, particularly if there are statistical or contentious issues to consider. Each journal has its own web page where information can be found about the scope of the journal, and the process for submitting manuscripts for consideration and for subscribing to the journal.

Universities subscribe to thousands of journals as part of their provision for staff and students. Traditionally, journals were found in a separate section of the library, where new issues were added to the shelves each time they were issued. However, the computer revolution has had a major impact on information dissemination. Nowadays, journals are available electronically via the Internet. Universities and other organisations subscribe each year to defined sets ('bundles') of journals through agreements with the publishers. The range of journals to which they subscribe will change slightly each year, particularly as new journals are created. Your university library will have induction sessions to introduce students to the electronic journal catalogue as well as to the increasing range of other resources available.

Occasionally, you may want to obtain a copy of an article that is in a journal to which your university does not currently subscribe. In that case you should go to the librarian and ask if he or she can obtain a copy for you. In the UK, paper copies of less readily available journal articles are posted from the British Library in York. The actual cost of this must be at least £10 per article, so you may need the signature of a member of academic staff. The librarian will no doubt check to see whether he or she can retrieve the article electronically even if you have been unable to do so. From experience, journals that are not available electronically in universities tend to be more local in readership, and to publish research that is less rigorous and less generalisable. Unless you are studying a localised topic it is unlikely that you will need to venture much from the journals available electronically.

Bibliographic databases

As the volume of published research adds continually to the store of human knowledge, the task of identifying relevant material gets increasingly difficult. To assist in this retrieval process, bibliographic databases have been created. These bibliographic databases contain primarily collections of the abstract (summary) and reference for articles published in a range of journals relevant to the focus of that database. The databases contain (in varying degrees) mechanisms to facilitate searching these abstracts for your topic of interest, which will be discussed below.

The development of bibliographic databases accessible through the Internet has transformed the process of retrieving relevant research on a topic. A much higher quality search can be achieved than when relying on looking through printed documents (Taylor, 2003).

There is no one major database that one might regard as a primary source for identifying social work research, perhaps because we are such an eclectic discipline or perhaps because of limited investment from governments or our 'industry' bodies. Therefore, a number of databases are often used to search for material in social work, such as those illustrated. Universities and many social work employers subscribe to these databases. The databases available for searching are steadily evolving in terms of their scope and facilities.

Research Summary

Bibliographic databases (as at summer 2015)

- *Scopus:* This is currently the largest bibliographic database, containing over 49 million records abstracted from over 20,000 peer-reviewed journals across all academic subject areas. On such a diverse database it is particularly important to consider whether people outside your field will use search terms with different meanings.
- *MEDLINE:* This is a very large, international database published by the US National Library of Medicine. It contains over 19 million records abstracted from over 5,500 peer-reviewed journals including high quality social work journals. It is good for social work topics that interface with medicine (e.g. child protection, mental health, elder care) but less useful for a topic in criminal justice, community development or disability viewed primarily in functional or social terms. Provided on the OVID platform, it is one of the highest quality databases from a user perspective.
- *PsycINFO:* This is a large, international database published by the American Psychological Association. It contains over 3 million records from 2,500 peer-reviewed journals including many of relevance to social work, particularly where we are interested in experimental studies that might provide evidence to underpin practice, or research involving psycho-social constructs such as 'self-esteem', 'stress' or 'resilience'. Provided on the OVID platform, it is one of the highest quality databases from a user perspective.
- *Cumulative Index to Nursing & Allied Health Literature (CINAHL):* This is a large, international database of nearly 3 million records that abstracts from about 3,000 peer-reviewed journals, including many of interest to social work. As with MEDLINE, it is good for topics that interface with healthcare. Disability topics may be found more easily by searching for particular conditions.
- *Social Science Citation Index (SSCI)* in *Web of Knowledge:* This is a large, international database for the social sciences covering about 2,500 peer-reviewed journals. It has a 'citation searching' feature which enables you to access readily the references within an article that

(Continued)

(Continued)

you retrieve if they are also on this database. However, you should note that it has no indexing system (see below) which limits its ease of use for thorough searching on a topic.

- *Applied Social Sciences Index and Abstracts (ASSIA):* This is a moderate-sized database which contains nearly 400,000 records abstracted from 500 peer-reviewed journals covering a range of social sciences.
- *Social Services Abstracts (SSA):* This is a moderate-sized, USA-based database that contains about 200,000 records, abstracting from about 1,300 peer-reviewed journals in the field of social work, human services, social welfare, social policy and community development.
- *Health Management Information Consortium (HMIC):* This is a moderate-sized UK database abstracting peer-reviewed journals on health and social care management. It contains about 300,000 records.
- *Social Care Online:* This is the national database provided by the UK Social Care Institute for Excellence as part of its mission to improve social care services by disseminating knowledge. It covers nearly 700 peer-reviewed journals related to social care (including social work) and contains about 200,000 records. It is useful for material that is specific to UK policies, services and concepts.
- *Criminal Justice Abstracts:* This is a moderate-sized database including over 200,000 records from the most relevant sources for criminal justice.
- *National Criminal Justice Reference Service Abstracts:* This moderate-sized, USA-based database contains over 200,000 records related to criminal justice, including juvenile justice and drug control.
- *Social Work Abstracts (SWA):* This is a small database published by the National Association of Social Workers in the USA, and is frequently not available in UK universities. It contains about 75,000 records and covers about 500 peer-reviewed journals relevant to social work.
- *LexisNexis:* This provides consolidated and annotated UK legislation consisting of over 86,000 enactments dating back to 1266 and access to over 600,000 case law documents. Approximately 7,000 transcripts and 2,000 handed-down judgments are added each year.
- *Westlaw UK:* This provides 400,000 case law reports and transcripts back to 1220, and legislation consolidated back to 1267, which is updated daily. It abstracts over 110 journals and provides access to abstracts of every article in every English-language legal journal in Europe via the *Legal Journals Index*.

A number of Internet platforms have been created, such as *Web of Knowledge*, *OVID SP*, *EBSCOhost* and *Proquest Complete*, which enable simultaneous searching across a number of databases. These might be described as 'meta-search engines', and are useful for a 'quick and dirty' search. However, these meta-search engines have limited usefulness for rigorous searching as they are attempting to search across databases that have different indexing systems (see below) without matching the search to the indexing terminology. For high quality searching through such platforms, you need to switch off ('unclick') the meta-search engine so that you can search each database separately.

Publishers of journals (who often publish books also) are increasingly providing systems for searching the range of journals that they publish. The methods explained here for searching 'independent' databases (such as in the list above) are also relevant for these 'publisher databases' but the limitation in terms of the journals that they cover needs to be noted. As publications of interest to social work come from a range of publishers, we do not consider these explicitly here, although the principles of searching still apply in limited form. Our focus is on databases that are provided independently of journal publishers.

Grey literature

One question that you will need to address at an early stage of your review of research is whether or not to include **grey literature**. This is a term that is used to apply to any publication that is not controlled by a commercial publisher. In practice, it is used to mean papers that are not reviewed by anonymous, **masked** reviewers with expertise in the field. Grey literature includes conference papers, organisation reports and news-sheets as well as theses and dissertations produced as part of academic studies. In favour of excluding grey literature is the argument that the highest quality research will be published in peer-reviewed journals. This therefore acts as some guarantor of quality for the person who is less knowledgeable on the detail of research methods as it will have been peer-reviewed by colleagues who are knowledgeable in the field. Journal publication ensures a high standard of reporting of both methods and results. In favour of including grey literature is the argument that there may be commercial or political pressures not to publish material more widely, particularly if the study produced results that might be embarrassing to established political or organisational interests or which show that an intervention is not effective. Another argument for including grey literature is that there is sometimes a time lag in material reaching a journal. Note, however, that this time lag is primarily related to the improved quality brought about by the peer-review process, so to some extent this is a trade-off between timeliness and assurance of quality. If you do decide to include grey literature you will need to show how you intend to access this as it is generally not included in the major databases listed above.

Resource Summary

Databases for grey literature

- *OpenGrey* database (www.opengrey.eu) specialises in abstracting grey literature (previously called SIGLE).
- *BASE*, the Bielefeld Academic Search Engine (www.base-search.net), is another source for grey literature (the advanced search allows exclusion of books and articles).
- *The British Library* (ethos.bl.uk) provides access to UK theses.
- *DART* Europe (dart-europe.eu) provides access to a range of international e-theses.

Internet searching

A more recent development is the use of search engines (such as GoogleScholar, Yahoo, Bing, Ask, etc.) to search for research (see the example in Figure 4.1). Nowadays, each journal has a website on which it puts information about each article published. This usually includes the reference and abstract free, even if there is a charge to access the full text. In principle, therefore, these Internet search engines should be able to retrieve at least the reference and abstract of any article published. Comparative studies of the effectiveness of Internet search engines against bibliographic databases have been carried out (Bergman, 2012; Best et al., 2014b; Chen, 2006; Falagas et al., 2007; McFadden et al., 2012; McGinn et al., 2014). These studies suggest that although Internet search engines are good enough to include alongside searching bibliographic databases, they generally retrieve only a modest fraction of the relevant articles available. One might surmise that in order to cope with the vast amount of data potentially available, the algorithm used to determine which 'hits' to show is ruthless in trying to exclude anything which might possibly be irrelevant to the extent of excluding many relevant items. The main drawback with Internet search engines is the fact that the user has very limited control of the search. The logic of the algorithm used to identify which items to show as 'hits' is not within the control of the user, and the rules may be changed by the provider of the search engine at any time, often without notice.

Review Concept

Professional judgements regarding adults at risk of abuse

MEDLINE: ('adult protection' OR 'elder abuse' OR 'elder mistreatment' OR 'vulnerable adult' OR 'elder neglect') AND (decision* OR judg*ment OR factor* OR indicator*)

Social Care Online: ('adult protection' OR 'elder abuse' OR 'elder mistreatment' OR 'vulnerable adult*' OR 'elder neglect') AND freetext ('decision*' OR 'judg*ment*' OR "factor*" OR "indicator*')

Figure 4.1 A rigorous search including an Internet search (from Killick and Taylor, 2009) (NB: the terminology of the search is explained below)

The major weakness with Internet search engines such as these is that the algorithm used to determine which 'hits' appear is a closely guarded commercial secret. Thus, the user cannot determine or know clearly what is happening. However, in general the principles for searching bibliographic databases explained below are a useful guide to how to go about searching on the Internet. This is clearly a growing area of development (Bergman, 2012) and it is likely that over the next few years the search engines and bibliographic databases will learn from each other and implement additional features to help users.

Systematic searching

Index-term and text-term searching

Most of the databases mentioned above have an indexing system such that each abstract added is indexed against the standard set of terms (thesaurus) adopted by that database. The main exception for our purposes is the Social Science Citation Index within the Web of Knowledge. You will probably find that some but not all your concepts are captured reasonably by the index terms on the database (**index-term searching**). If index terms are available on the database, then you can use those to express the relevant concept in your search. If your search involves a concept that does not correspond reasonably to an index term on a particular database, then you must use **text-term searching**, which means instructing the database to search in the titles and abstracts of articles for specific words that you identify. The availability of index terms greatly simplifies the process of constructing an effective search (see the example in Figure 4.2).

Review Concept

Residential homes for group living of older people

- *MEDLINE*: use MeSH (Medical Subject Heading) index term: Homes for the aged/
- *Social Science Citation Index* (which does not have an indexing system): use text terms: 'care home' OR 'institutional care' OR 'old people's home' OR 'old peoples home' OR 'residential care' OR 'home for the aged' OR 'homes for the aged' OR 'out of home care'

Figure 4.2   Example of capturing concepts with index terms

If there is no index term corresponding to your concept, you cannot use index-term searching and must use text-term searching. In this case you will need to identify the possible alternative words that might be used by an author of an article to express that concept. It is important that you do not think only of your own preferred term or what is regarded as acceptable in your society. Terms vary over time and across countries and cultures; your task is to retrieve any relevant articles on the chosen topic regardless of terminology of the time, place and culture. In particular you need to be aware of terminology that is unique to your culture or jurisdiction. For example 'looked after children' is a term used almost exclusively in the UK; authors in most countries would use a term such as 'children in care' or 'children in state care'.

Some concepts cannot be expressed effectively in a search formula, either by index terms or text terms. Concepts such as 'effects of' and 'effectiveness of' are frequently omitted for this reason, and also because such terms are often omitted from titles of articles. Concepts such as 'experiences of' or 'perceptions of' are also often omitted, although the section below on filters and search strings gives pointers on this.

Techniques for text-term searching

You have perhaps been wondering what to do about different parts of speech, word endings and variant spellings when undertaking text-term searching. Most databases have a system for truncation to enable multiple variations of a word root to be searched for at once. This enables the user to represent a number of alternative letters with a symbol – usually an asterisk (*), but sometimes a question mark (?) or a dollar sign ($) (see Figure 4.3). However, a computer will only retrieve what it is told to retrieve; it cannot 'understand' that 'adolescent' has anything to do with 'teenager' or that 'teach' is connected etymologically with 'taught'.

---

*Child** WILL RETRIEVE: *child, children, child's, children's, etc.*

*counsel** WILL RETRIEVE: *counsellor, counselor, counsellors, counselling, etc.*

*disab** WILL RETRIEVE: *disabled, disablement, disability, disabilities*

*institution** WILL RETRIEVE: *institution, institutional, institutions*

*social work** WILL RETRIEVE: *social work, social worker, social workers*

*teach** WILL RETRIEVE: *teacher, teachers, teaching* (BUT NOT *taught* !!!)

Figure 4.3 Illustrations of using truncation

Similarly, most databases have a system of 'wild cards' (usually the same symbols as for truncation) that can be used to represent any letter or no letter within a word. For example, *organi*ation* will retrieve both *organisation* and *organization*; *colo*r* will retrieve both *color* and *colour*.

You will have noticed in some of the above examples that quotation marks ('') have been used. These are to mark out phrases, instructing the database to retrieve these words only where they occur in this set phrase but not otherwise. If the words of a phrase are put into the search without speech marks, then the database will treat each one as a separate concept joined by 'AND'. You are likely to retrieve more irrelevant items. Their use makes the search more precise (see Figure 4.4). Historically, truncation and wild cards could not be used within speech marks for phrases. However, on some databases this is now possible. The database 'Help' menu and a librarian can assist.

'young offender' OR 'juvenile crime' OR 'juvenile delinquency'

Figure 4.4 Illustrations of the use of quotation marks

Abbreviations are in common use for some concepts and organisations. Sometimes articles will use common abbreviations in the abstract or title rather than the full word. Therefore, it is recommended that you use both the abbreviated and the full version of common abbreviations, joined by 'OR' within the brackets for that concept group of course. For example:

- (ASD OR Autism Spectrum Disorder);

- (CVA OR cardiovascular accident OR stroke);

- (HRA OR Human Rights Act);

- (LAC OR Looked After Children);

- (UNESCO OR United Nations Educational, Scientific and Cultural Organisation);

- (WHO OR World Health Organisation).

Databases update their index terms periodically to keep abreast of developments in knowledge. However, you will recognise that there is a balance to be struck. If the index terms are changed too often, users will feel lost when they are searching. If index terms are not revised sufficiently often to keep pace with expanding areas of knowledge, their usefulness in facilitating a search will reduce if many articles are indexed under the same heading.

Concept groups

Traditional literature reviews relied on a rather hit-and-miss process. As a student, your supervisor or a librarian might point you towards some key articles or books. As an academic, you might have asked experienced colleagues perhaps at a conference or your own institution. You would then have looked at those items to identify references within them to other publications and identify key authors in the field. You might use some manual method of searching the index of back issues of key journals to try to find other articles on your topic, keeping your eye open for material by the key authors you have already identified. This process is prone to bias and error. It is prone to the bias of the student and supervisor in terms of their existing knowledge and the avenues on which they embarked in terms of key journals and authors. It is prone to error in that the manual scanning of journal contents could easily miss an item.

The essential principle for developing a search on bibliographic databases is that you want to retrieve as many relevant items as possible while avoiding as far as possible retrieving irrelevant items (Taylor, 2003). For this purpose, your search question as discussed in Chapter 3 must be translated into clear concepts that can be used to construct a database search. Essentially, the concepts reflect the main aspects of your topic. The first task is to identify the main concepts within the question and to give these a name for your own convenience.

1. *Question*: Why do older people fall within residential or nursing homes?
   CONCEPT GROUPS: ‹older people› AND ‹falls› AND ‹institutional care›

2. *Question*: How often are social workers assaulted at work?
   CONCEPT GROUPS: ‹social worker› AND ‹violence›

3. *Question*: What effect does disclosure of childhood sexual abuse have on the family?
   CONCEPT GROUPS: ‹disclose› AND ‹sexual abuse› AND ‹family›

Figure 4.5 An example of identifying concept groups

The essential point is that we are interested only in articles that contain all the concepts that we have identified. Thus, in the first example in Figure 4.5, we are not interested in other aspects of older people in institutional care, such as nutrition or care regimes, for example, but only in falls. It is important to note that the concepts you are defining are those that are most appropriate for your particular purpose. For example, there are differences between residential homes and nursing homes in terms of admission criteria, registration requirements, staffing, etc. However, it may be that for your purpose – an interest in older people falling in such settings due to the flooring used – they form one homogeneous concept of institutional care. Sometimes the identification of concepts might seem ambiguous. In the second example in Figure 4.5, the search concepts would be equally valid to retrieve articles on violence *by* social workers as violence *to* social workers. It is not realistic to put the concept of 'to' or 'by' into a database search and any spurious articles will have to be rejected by hand from the hits retrieved. Typically, two to four concepts are required for useful database searches on social work topics. A visual illustration of combining concept groups is given in Figure 4.6. Combining two concepts with the operator 'AND' is a way of narrowing the search to include only those articles that include both concepts. Similarly, joining three concepts with each other by 'AND' narrows the search to articles that include all three concepts.

In order to express these alternative terms for a concept we use the **Boolean algebra** operator 'OR'. This is used to link words or terms within a concept group. It means

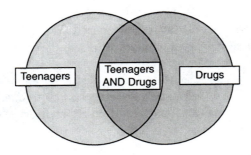

Figure 4.6   Visual illustration of combining concepts using 'AND'

in effect that we do not mind which of these words are used to represent that concept, because our aim is to retrieve all articles on the topic regardless of the particular terminology preference of particular authors, journals, cultures or countries. When joined by 'OR', an article (in its title or abstract) may contain any of these terms (or more than one of them) for it to be acceptable in relation to that particular concept. A visual illustration of combining terms, which for your purposes capture the same concept, is given in Figure 4.7. The way that you express this operator varies between databases; in this text we will use capitalised 'OR' to indicate that it is a database operator that carries out a specific function in combining equivalent terms within concepts in this way.

CONCEPT: *learning disability*

CAPTURING ALTERNATIVE TERMINOLOGY:

('intellectual disability' OR 'intellectual impairment' OR 'learning difficulty' OR 'learning disability' OR 'mental handicap')

Figure 4.7   Example of alternative terms for text-term searching

The crucial issue, then, is how we combine the use of 'AND' and 'OR' within an effective search. For our last and most important acknowledgement of Boolean algebra, I need to remind you of what you learnt in school about the use of brackets within an equation, although I hasten to add that we are using words not numbers. What is in the brackets must be treated as a meaningful entity in itself ('do what is in the brackets first') before combining this with what is outside the brackets. We put terms expressing a particular concept linked by 'OR' within brackets. Each concept is within its own brackets and we join the concepts (sets of brackets) with 'AND'. This is easiest seen with an example, such as in Figure 4.8.

- (foster care OR fostering service) AND (breakdown OR disruption)
- (mental health OR mental illness OR psychiatric) AND (involuntary OR compulsory OR compel OR detain)
- (child welfare OR child protection OR child abuse OR child neglect) AND (assess OR decision OR decide OR judgement OR judgment OR significant harm OR registration OR register)
- (racism OR racist OR ethnic) AND (attitude* OR belief* or prejudice) AND employment OR job OR work)

See Taylor and Killick (2013) for a fuller example.

Figure 4.8   Illustrations of combining concepts using brackets

When you are combining the terms within a database search, it will be useful if you can remember this basic algebraic tenet of ensuring that what is in the brackets is meaningful. Within each bracket you can include as many equivalent terms as you think necessary to capture that particular concept. Note that it does not matter for the resulting search what order is used for concept groups or for terms within concept groups. What is essential is that equivalent terms (for our purpose) are within brackets connected by 'OR' and that concept groups themselves are joined by 'AND'. On some databases – such as those on the OVID platform – you enter terms in successive rows and then combine them. On some databases you enter the string of terms joined by the operators 'AND', 'OR' and brackets () using the above logic. A form to assist with this structuring of concepts and terms is provided in Appendix 4. The form is designed such that terms that mean the same thing for the purposes of your review are included within one of the boxes. The boxes (each containing a concept) are joined by 'AND' on the form. The terms within each box are, of course, each joined by 'OR'. The boxes have been given curved corners as an aid to remembering that the terms within each box are expressed as being within brackets when it comes to creating a search on a database. The brackets, as you can see, are then joined by the operator 'AND'.

Activity 4.1

Using brackets and terms correctly

What is the difference between these two searches? They have the same terms in the same sequence, but the brackets are positioned differently.

- (older people) AND (Alzheimer's OR dementia)
- (older people AND Alzheimer's) OR (dementia)

The first search is meaningful and useful. We are interested in articles that refer to dementia or to Alzheimer's in relation to older people. The second search will retrieve articles on Alzheimer's in relation to older people and articles on dementia with any age group. There is no sound logic to this second search.

The concepts that you have identified are combined by using the operator 'AND' (derived from Boolean algebra) when you put these into a database search. This is a way of expressing algebraically that we require all the concepts to be present for the abstract of that article to be retrieved by the search as a 'hit'. The way that you express this operator varies between databases; in this text we will use capitalised 'AND' to indicate that it is a database operator that carries out a specific function in combining concepts in this way. Each database has a 'Help' function which will tell you about the symbols to use for the various techniques outlined in this chapter. Appendix 4 contains a template to assist in laying out your search clearly. Each of the rectangles contains one concept; within the rectangle insert words with similar meaning joined by 'OR'. The rectangles are joined by 'AND' to illustrate the way of joining concepts. The rectangles have been given curved corners to remind you that when you write the search formula in full, the synonyms joined by 'OR' are contained within brackets; each bracketed concept in then joined by 'AND'.

If you have a review question about the effectiveness of an intervention and are using the PICO search structure explained in Chapter 3, then each row of the PICO acronym is joined by 'AND', and the terms used within each row are joined by 'OR', as illustrated in the box below. However, it should be noted that this structure is often of limited value for structuring a search on effectiveness of social care at the present time as there are relatively few experimental studies of interventions, so we are unlikely to specify a particular comparator on many occasions. Similarly, we may want to retrieve studies with a range of outcome measures rather than specifying these at the start.

Review Summary

Use of PICO search structure

Question: Is cognitive behavioural therapy effective for young offenders with drug addiction problems?

Population: ('antisocial behavio*r' OR 'behaviour disorder*' OR 'conduct disorder' OR 'juvenile delinquen*' OR 'juvenile justice' OR 'young offend*' OR 'youth crime' OR 'youth justice')

AND

Intervention: ('aggression replacement training' OR 'behavio*r therapy' OR 'cognitive behavio*r therapy' OR 'cognitive therapy' OR 'cognitive training' OR 'dialectical behaviour therapy')

AND

Comparator: ‹this category is blank as the review did not specify any particular alternative intervention for comparison›

AND

Outcome: (rehabilitat* OR reoffend* OR 'out-of-home placement*' OR 'sexual behavio*r problem*' OR 'mental health' OR 'mental illness')

(Adapted from Campbell et al., 2010)

Filters and search strings

The better databases provide mechanisms to filter the hits to improve precision of searching. Some provide a filter for 'research', which is useful to separate empirical papers from theoretical and ideological papers, and other material in journals such as editorials which also may be abstracted. Some, such as MEDLINE, have filters for stages of studies (trials) of effectiveness of interventions. The search strings illustrated in Figure 4.9 are useful to add as an additional concept group where filters are not available to refine the search by question or method.

> - Questions about experiences (qualitative): (attitude* OR experience* OR opinion* OR perception* OR perspectives* OR satisf* OR view*) [see Fisher et al., 2006]
> - Questions about effectiveness (experimental): (effect* OR impact* OR outcome* OR 'treatment outcome')

Figure 4.9 Search strings to identify articles by research question and methods

The database may have a filter to allow you to limit the number of years back to search. The default will be to search back as far as the database records. This varies greatly. Most databases commenced operation about the middle 1980s. However, MEDLINE includes records back to 1946 and PsycINFO back to 1806! In terms of your final search, this facility is helpful in prompting you to consider the date range for your literature review. Do you want it to be 'up to the present' or does it make more sense to cut off at the end of the last calendar year? Do you want to go as far back on each particular database as it will allow (i.e. a different date range on each database) or does it make more sense for this particular literature review to have a defined earliest publication date? If you run your search in February, you can probably be confident nowadays that databases have abstracted from all relevant journals for the previous year.

Hand searching, citation searching and expert contact

Despite the sophistication of constructing careful searches of bibliographic databases, do not be deluded into thinking that you are likely to achieve a massively sensitive search with virtually no irrelevant articles. Unfortunately, this is not the case! Database searching will provide a much more comprehensive and less biased selection of relevant articles than the traditional hit-and-miss approaches. However, irrelevant articles will still be retrieved. But even if the database searching retrieves only half the relevant articles potentially available, it is still much more rigorous and less biased that relying only on hand searching approaches, which are likely to achieve far fewer. To be more thorough, citation searching, hand searching and expert contact (as discussed below) can be used to complement database searching.

Citation searching is getting references from relevant articles already retrieved by reading through the list at the end of the article. Citation searching is a facility provided within an increasing number of bibliographic databases whereby the user can look up articles (if available through the same database) that have cited this article. Traditionally, the Social Science Citation Index (within Web of Knowledge) was the most relevant database for our purposes that had this feature. Increasingly, however, other databases such as MEDLINE are adding citation searching features. Note that this citation searching will only be to other cited articles that are abstracted on to that same database. In the present context, citation searching means particularly looking through the reference list at the end of each relevant article retrieved to see whether there are any titles that look relevant, and worth looking up the abstract.

Hand searching includes activities such as looking at journal contents lists for recent years to see what titles seem to be relevant, again then looking at the abstract of any that appear from the title to be relevant.

Expert contact, which refers to contacting eminent authors in the field to ask if they have published anything relevant, is much easier in this era of emails and publicly available email addresses for academic staff of universities, who are generally the most prolific authors of research articles. The 'experts' may be the authors of the relevant articles that you have retrieved, or you may have some other approach to defining who to contact such as membership of a learned society or conference.

It is important if you are going to be systematic about your search that you have a methodology or criteria for using citation searching, hand searching and expert contact if you decide to use these to complement database searching. Define your criteria at the start of the exercise and then apply those criteria. An example in relation to hand searching might be to define which journals with some rationale and how many years back to search these. An example in relation to expert contact might be to contact only authors of articles deemed relevant by your database search.

Processes of developing a search

Sequence of terms

It does not matter in what order you enter the concepts on to a bibliographic database (unlike with most search engines) in terms of the final search outcome. However, for the purposes of developing your search I would advise that you enter first the best established concepts – i.e. those that are most likely to have index terms. Then work towards the least clearly defined concepts – i.e. those where you are likely to have to use text-term searching. Checking on the hits retrieved as you go along will give you some idea of whether you are on the right track. You may find that on some databases the index terms available enable you to combine two of your concepts whereas on other databases they do not – for example, you may have a concept about families and another concept about conflicts that occur within families. On some databases it may be that there is an index term such as 'family relationships' that covers two of the concepts that you have structured in your search.

Advanced searching – testing new terms with operator 'NOT'

Some databases have a function 'NOT' which enables the user to exclude items that contain whatever follows the NOT. This may be an index term or text term. Thus, for example, 'community care' NOT 'mental health' will identify articles on community care but not those that refer to mental health. There may be more than one term before or after the 'NOT', such as ('community care' OR 'NHS and Community Care Act') NOT ('mental health' OR 'mental illness') which would have a similar outcome. The use of 'NOT' within a search formula needs a note of caution. It may exclude articles because the words after the 'NOT' are included almost incidentally in the abstract. However, the operator 'NOT' (where available) is very useful during the stages of developing a search formula. Thus, for example, '(co-ownership housing OR housing association* OR housing scheme*) NOT (co-ownership housing OR housing association*)' will identify the number of additional articles that have been retrieved by including the term 'housing scheme*'. In algebraic language this can be written as '(A or B or C) not (A or B)' as a formula to test the impact of adding term 'C' to an existing search involving 'A or B'. This method can be repeated for each new term being considered, with any number of terms in the existing formula (Taylor, 2003).

Use of date limit

The date limit you use for your search will depend on aspects of your question, as discussed in Chapter 3. In relation to the process of constructing your search, it may be useful to remember that the amount of time that it takes a database to search can generally be reduced by limiting the number of years searched. When you are developing your search and testing out new terms, you may feel frustrated at the time that the database takes to return the 'hits' so that you can see how well your latest search is performing. By limiting the search during this developmental phase to a more restricted date range (e.g. the past five years, or the past year if there are many publications) you may speed up your process of developing the search.

Recording your search

It will be apparent by now that the construction and execution of a search is a detailed exercise that requires knowledge, skill and care. It is an art as well as a science. It is important that you document what you have done in creating and carrying out your search, as evidence of rigour in this aspect of reviewing the literature. You should record the databases used, the basic structure of concept groups employed, the search terms used within each concept, and the date on which the searches were run.

Quality of searching

As more relevant search terms are added within a concept group, the number of relevant articles retrieved will increase. However, by the nature of the database, adding more terms will almost certainly also increase the number of irrelevant hits retrieved by the search. The quality of a database search can be considered along these two dimensions: sensitivity and precision. *Sensitivity* is the fraction of the total available articles that are retrieved by a search on a particular database. *Precision* is the ability of a search to retrieve only relevant items – that is, to exclude irrelevant items (Taylor, 2003). Thus, if a particular database retrieves 10 relevant hits out of 100 relevant hits retrieved in total across all searching, then that database has a sensitivity of 10/100 = 10 per cent. If in retrieving these 10 relevant hits the database turns up a total of 50 hits, then its precision is 10/50 = 20 per cent. For further discussion about database searching, see Best et al. (2014b), McFadden et al. (2012), McGinn et al. (2014), Taylor (2009), Taylor et al. (2003) and Taylor et al. (2007b)

Even with a thorough process such as described here, you must expect to retrieve many irrelevant hits in the process of retrieving relevant items. It does not take too long to skim down a list of titles (first of all) and then through the abstracts to eliminate those that are obviously irrelevant. If your search retrieves too many relevant hits for your topic, you can make the topic more focused by adding an additional concept group. If your search retrieves too few relevant hits, then either you need to identify additional terms within the concept groups or else your search is too narrow in relation to the volume of articles published on the topic. In this latter case, removing a concept group will broaden the search and more articles will be retrieved.

Data extraction

There are various options for managing the results of your search. Typically, you can email the results to yourself from the database. This is normally provided with a feature where you can make a few notes in the title and body of the email, such as to remind you of which search it is for which the results are attached. With the better databases, you can download the hits directly into software for managing references such as RefWorks, on which a university librarian will be able to advise.

The databases we are considering focus on including abstracts of articles. The abstract should be enough to determine whether that article is relevant for your review, although sadly the quality of some abstracts leaves much to be desired. If you are unsure about whether an article is relevant, you will have to look at the full text, for which you will need to use whatever system is available in the university. Normally, journal articles are available electronically also.

In order to extract the key elements from the article, it is recommended that you skim read first to get an overview. Look particularly at the abstract, statement of the purpose of the study and the conclusions. Ensure that you bear in mind your review question as you read; there will be many papers that are interesting, but rather fewer that are directly relevant. Extracting the key aspects of each study and tabulating these is an essential first step towards most types of synthesis. Typically, the following aspects are extracted and presented in a table.

- Author(s).

- Year.

- Country of the study.

- Research design.

- Intervention and outcome measures (if relevant).

- Study participants (and their setting) or other data source.

- Data collection method.

- Main findings.

Review Example

Study findings: extract from review on risk communication in dementia

First author, date, country	Design	Sample – participants	Data collection	Main findings
McDonald, 2010, UK	Qualitative, using grounded theory.	Purposive sample of 14 current cases of social workers working with older people with dementia living in the community.	Document review and semi-structured interviews re: current cases; asked to compare current case with similar case concluded before Mental Capacity Act 2005.	Three types of decision making in risk emerged: legalistic, actuarial and rights based. Tensions between approaches that participants thought they ought to take and those they did take. Inter-agency cases were more likely to prompt a legalistic approach: more defensive decision making.
Henry et al., 2009, Australia and New Zealand	Experiment with danger-rating tasks: faces and situations, and tests of emotion recognition.	106 community dwelling adults: 34 people with dementia; 38 people with mild cognitive impairment; 34 demographically matched control group.	Black and white photographs presented for judgement of approachability. Photos of social and recreational activities presented for judgement of dangerousness.	Dementia group had difficulty differentiating high from low danger situations which reflected a bias to over-attribute the level of threat posed by normatively judged non-threatening situations. This difficulty was related to more general cognitive decline.

(Adapted from Stevenson et al., 2014)

Completing such a table will require the reader to get to know the studies intimately. Completing the data collection table requires knowledge of research methods and how to appraise them against the research question – this is the focus of Chapters 5, 6 and 7.

Such a table is not a synthesis in itself, but is a way of presenting the key elements in summary form and structured in relation to each other. Generally, this table is presented in date order of studies for ease of retrieval and so that patterns of development over time (such as in terminology) might be more easily observed. If the studies are grouped together into categories for a **narrative synthesis** (see Chapter 8), the table might be restructured into two or three parts relating to the main categories within the overall topic. Note that this is more useful if there is little overlap in terms of studies contributing to more than one category. If there is this overlap, a way of recording this clearly will be required. If a study is summarised in more than one place (i.e. in the tables for more than one category), it will be essential to note this at the foot of each table to avoid any possibility of double-counting the number of studies included in the overall review.

The process of extracting data and tabulating the main characteristics of studies leads to a consideration of the rigour of the studies retrieved, as discussed in the next three chapters.

Becoming a social worker

Being confident in searching bibliographic databases has become an essential foundational skill for any professional in this digital age. Once you have a clear and answerable question, the next task is to translate that into a search on a database. This chapter relates particularly to domain 5.1 of the PCF on awareness of new research, and explains how to become skilled in identifying relevant research on topics related to your area of practice.

Reflection Point

What challenges do you face personally in using a computer to search bibliographic databases to find relevant research?

How can you address your learning needs and any practical barriers?

Activity 4.2

Evidence into practice task

Using your practice-focused question:

1. Select either MEDLINE or PsycINFO database.
2. Construct a search formula for your practice evidence question, using the advice of a librarian as appropriate.
3. Ensure that you record the search formula used as well as saving the hits retrieved in a systematic way (e.g. into Refworks or email to yourself).

Chapter Summary

- Knowledge and skills in searching bibliographic databases are essential for any professional in order to maintain their up-to-date knowledge of research in their field of practice.
- Journal articles are the main avenue by which research is published.
- Bibliographic databases provide a ready and thorough means to search for relevant research.
- Internet search engines are useful but do not instil confidence because they provide limited information about the search process to the user.
- Construction of a meaningful search requires an understanding of basic principles of how the databases use 'AND' and 'OR'. This is simple once explained.
- Databases contain a number of facilities to assist in effective searching, including truncation, wild cards and filters.
- The quality of a search may be judged primarily in terms of sensitivity and precision.
- It is important to record details of your search: date, databases used and search formula used on each.

Further Reading

Campbell Collaboration (C2): www.campbellcollaboration.org

The Social Welfare Coordinating Group of the Campbell Collaboration oversees systematic reviews of effectiveness on social welfare and gives advice on database searching to those undertaking reviews. The principles in this book are in accord with those used in the Cochrane and Campbell Collaborations, but techniques here are at a simplified level.

Cochrane Collaboration (CC): www.cochrane.org

Review groups of the Cochrane Collaboration oversee systematic reviews of effectiveness related to a particular topic area, such as the Dementia and Cognitive Improvement Group and the Developmental, Psychosocial and Learning Problems Group (www.cochranelibrary.com/about/cochrane-review-groups.html). These review groups give advice on database searching to those undertaking reviews.

Social Care Institute for Excellence (SCIE): www.scie.org.uk

SCIE improves the lives of people who use care services by sharing knowledge about what works, in particular by providing an online database (Social Care Online), commissioning systematic reviews, and producing resources that summarise key messages for good practice. SCIE has produced a guide on systematic literature reviewing which includes advice on database searching.

Taylor, BJ, Dempster, M and Donnelly, M (2003) Hidden gems: Systematically searching electronic databases for research publications for social work and social care. *British Journal of Social Work,* 33 (4): 423–39.

This article outlines pioneering principles of database searching in social work, and ways in which the quality of searching may be measured.

Chapter 5

Appraising surveys

Introduction

The survey is one of the most commonly used methods of gathering data from an entire group or a subsection of that group. We are constantly bombarded by letters, telephone calls, emails and texts asking for our demographics, our experience or our opinions. Surveys are popular because they are a relatively simple and effective means to explore concepts, describe populations or explain the relationship between two factors. Survey methods, like other forms of research, are subject to error but careful design and implementation can enhance validity and reliability. Before accepting survey findings or applying them to practice, the reader must be sure that they have been gathered and analysed correctly. This chapter will describe the key components of the survey method and discuss the ways in which surveys can be used. It will suggest ways in which the quality of a survey can be appraised and it will present a critical appraisal tool that can be applied to survey-based research.

The chapter goes on to consider in turn the ten quality appraisal questions as outlined in the QAT-S: Quality Appraisal Tool: Survey research in Appendix 1. It provides some general aspects of research appraisal that have relevance to Chapters 6 and 7. Most of the points in this chapter about survey methods apply equally to extraction of data from files, whether paper or electronic.

What is a survey?

The term 'survey' has been attributed a number of meanings, which can lead to confusion. Some use the term to describe any questioning process while others consider surveys to be any paper-based form of data collection. In research terms a survey can be described as follows:

> *A survey is a method of asking an agreed series of questions of a subset of a population, to gather information that can be analysed to describe specific characteristics of the total population.*

In many cases the questions are asked of individual respondents via interview, online survey or paper questionnaire. However, the quality measures discussed in this chapter can equally be used to appraise studies of secondary data.

Research Example

Survey using secondary data

The aim of this study was to establish the incidence of suicidal ideation and behaviour amongst young people (age 16–21 years) leaving state care in one Health and Social Care Trust in Northern Ireland, and to explore the correlation between this and client risk factors that might inform professional practice. Data were gathered from 164 case files of the total 215 (response rate 76%) in relation to all open cases as of 30 April 2012 extracted by the relevant social workers through the use of a standard data collection tool.

(Hamilton et al., 2015)

This chapter will assist in the appraisal of surveys that comply with the following requirements:

- the research relates to a defined population e.g. social work students;

- the entire population (**census**) or a subset (**sample**) are engaged in the study;

- the method is primarily quantitative – e.g. age, gender, number of clients; or

- data is gathered primarily through the use of questions – e.g. telephone interview.

Fowler (1995) argues that each step in survey design can improve or reduce the accuracy of the study and the quality of the findings is only as good as the weakest part of the process. For this reason the reader must critically evaluate each aspect of the survey method before deciding on the credibility of the results.

When assessing the quality of a survey report the practitioner is considering the strength of its method and the credibility of its conclusions. McColl et al. have identified four key measures that form the basis of this chapter. A quality survey is:

- *valid:* measures the quantity or concept that is supposed to be measured;

- *reliable:* measures the quantity or concept in a consistent or reproducible manner;

- *unbiased:* measures the quantity or concept in a way that does not systematically under- or overestimate the true value; and

- *discriminating:* can distinguish adequately between respondents for whom the underlying level of the quantity or concept is different.

(McColl et al., 2001, p2)

Rationale

The first stage in evaluating a survey is to consider the background to the study. A well-written report will identify the research team and the role of its members. The reason for undertaking the study will be described and, if the study is part of an educational course or larger research project, the details will be provided. Very importantly the existing literature relating to this theme will be critically analysed to identify the existing knowledge base and the gaps that need to be filled. The methods used previously to investigate this theme should also be evaluated. If there is a limit to published material relating to the theme, this will be stated and the authors may seek to generalise findings from other disciplines or geographic locations. Often quantitative surveys are based on findings from more qualitative approaches. When assessing the impact of therapeutic work in residential child care, SCIE (Macdonald and Millen, 2012) conducted interviews with staff and young people. The themes from this qualitative work were incorporated into an online survey sent to a random sample of staff to test whether the themes were generalisable to the broader population.

At the outset of the study it is helpful to define the key themes being investigated. While some variables such as age and body mass are generally understood, many in the world of social work are ambiguous and therefore need to be explicitly described.

Research Example

Defining the concept

The conceptualisation of the term 'suicidal ideation and behaviour' was used to enable measurement of this concept, which was defined through the literature review process as 'a wide variety of behaviours that involve the intention of or actual self-harm, ranging from suicidal thoughts and gestures through to self-harm, attempted suicide and completed suicide'.

(O'Connor and Sheehy, 2000, p10)

The research question should flow logically from the background and literature review. This will clearly describe the intentions of the study and the specific aspects of the subject that are being investigated. A clear research design needs to be based on a clear research question and often the question is expanded into aims and objectives.

Finally, the background or rationale may describe why this study is important and its potential benefits to the knowledge base and professional practice. The ideal for good social work research is to engage with key stakeholders at each stage of the process, to ensure that there will be value, not just for the researcher but also for managers, practitioners and service users.

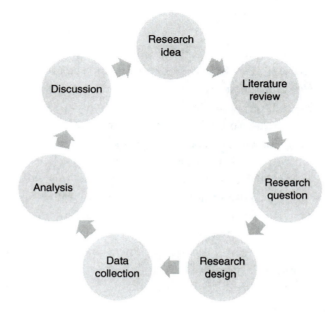

Figure 5.1 The research process

Basic research design

As Figure 5.1 shows, the logical flow of the design should be from the research question to the basic design. A key issue for survey research is the mode for administering the questions. The chosen mode should be justified and the potential strengths and weaknesses discussed.

Table 5.1 Modes for administering a survey

Self-completed	Interview-based	Survey of existing data source
Postal survey	Telephone interview	Case file survey
Online survey	Face-to-face	Electronic records
Mobile/text survey		

Figure 5.2 Theory of triple constraint in research design

Any research design will need to take into account the requirements in relation to time, cost and scope. It is rarely possible to produce highly accurate data on a large population in a short period of time. Bickman and Rog (2008) describe the necessary trade-off between these quality issues. This is illustrated by the theory of triple constraint used in the field of project management (Figure 5.2). Often research projects must tailor their design to the available time and funds. As a result, the scope and precision of the study may be limited. In the rationale, a survey report should state the constraints and justify the chosen design. A good report will explicitly state the strengths and limitations of the study often in the conclusions. Considering the impact of any limitations is a key component of research appraisal. Bickman and Rog (2008) outlined four issues when considering the impact of design trade-offs:

1. generalisability;

2. conclusiveness of findings;

3. precision of estimates; and

4. comprehensiveness of measurement.

A key issue for survey design is the selection of the respondent group. In most cases the respondents are service providers or recipients who have unique knowledge and expertise relating to the theme. It is possible that more than one group of respondents could be included, allowing triangulation of the different perspectives. A study of child protection case conferences may seek the views of parents, social workers and other professionals to give a balanced understanding of the process. Similarly, a core respondent group may need to be excluded for moral or practical reasons. A subject group may not wish to be involved in the study or it may be deemed to be unethical to ask specific questions. In evaluating research findings it is important to ask how able the chosen respondents are to answer the research question.

- Can retired social workers describe the pressures of today's workforce?

- Can family members describe the experience of older people in day centres?

Whatever the chosen mode of administration and respondent group, the research design should try to ensure that the mode of measurement is identical in every circumstance. Variation in administration can introduce additional factors that may distort the findings and limit the credibility of results.

Sampling strategy

Perhaps the most important factor in appraising the quality of quantitative survey-based research is the extent to which the respondents represent the focus population. This is less of an issue for qualitative exploratory studies that are primarily interested in meaning rather than measurement. In a census the survey includes all members of a population, but this is expensive for large groups and many surveys seek to select a subset or sample in such a way that the data will provide a credible estimate of the entire population. Ineffective sampling is one of the primary ways in which error can be introduced into a study. All samples introduce sampling error and good research will seek to reduce this to an acceptable level. If the sample is not properly selected, the findings cannot be related to a broader population. For this reason, researchers need to carefully describe three aspects of their study:

1. sampling method;

2. sample size; and

3. response rates.

Table 5.2 Methods of sampling

Total population	Probability (random) samples	Non-probability samples
Census	Simple random sample Stratified random sample Multistage sample Multiphase sample Cluster sample	Convenience sample Purposive or judgement sample Quota sample Snowball sample

A good survey using a **probability sample** should describe the total population that it seeks to study and the sample frame that was used. A sample frame is the total list of members of the population that the researchers plan to use. When studying social workers it might be the list of all practitioners registered with the Social Care Council on a specific date. When studying members of the public, it might be an electoral register. The sampling method is then used to select a smaller group of potential respondents. In some studies non-probability sampling methods are the only option or the most practical option. In these circumstances the report should recognise the potential dangers and justify the representativeness of their sample if they are generalising their findings to larger groups.

Having described the sampling frame and the sampling method, a survey report should state the size of the sample selected. A power analysis will calculate the necessary number of responses to allow findings to be generalised with some confidence. There is no correct percentage for a sample size but the researchers must take into account:

1. the size of the total population;

2. the expected response rate;

3. the margin of sampling error; and

4. the type of analysis that they plan to use.

In reality, the pragmatics of cost and time are often an additional factor but the reader should be cautious if the potential error is large or, worse, the power calculations are not shown.

The final important factor relating to sample size is the response rate. Few surveys obtain data from every member of the chosen sample and members of the public are increasingly likely to refuse to participate in a study if they see no benefit to themselves. Improving participation in research studies has become a science in itself and the report may outline the steps taken to maximise the number of returns. Those who choose not to participate in the study reduce the sample and therefore the accuracy of the study. More importantly, if non-returns come primarily from a specific group they will reduce the representativeness of the sample. This is known as response bias. In general, those who respond to surveys are the most motivated and articulate, which means that findings may be skewed towards the views of this group. Potentially, a large sample with a poor return rate is less useful than a small sample with a good return rate. In planning a project, researchers should try to anticipate potential non-returns and design their study accordingly.

Ethical issues

Surveys, like all aspects of social work practice, should promote the well-being of those who receive our services and it is therefore essential that the research process does not cause unnecessary pain or distress. The last decade has seen the introduction of strict requirements relating to research undertaken within universities and government agencies. Many non-government organisations have followed suit to ensure that the rights and information of service users are protected. In the UK, the Department of Health's Research Governance Framework outlined the responsibilities of various parties in research activities and implemented a process to scrutinise the ethics of all research involving NHS agencies, staff or service users. Studies that have received regional ethical approval can be deemed to have included safeguards in relation to the following aspects of research.

- *Data protection:* Information gathered for health or social care reasons cannot be used for any other purpose. It is therefore not acceptable to use contact details or other information for research purposes without the permission of the individual. Research teams need to work closely with service providers to ensure effective recruitment without breaching data protection regulations. Increasingly, government agencies will have a data guardian who will only release information in line with agreed guidelines.

- *Voluntary participation:* Individuals should only be participating in a survey if they wish to be involved. They should be informed that a decision not to participate will not affect their eligibility for services. Participants should also be informed that they can withdraw at any stage without repercussions.

- *Informed consent:* To consent to participation the individual must have all the necessary information in a form that they understand. Providing complex information in an accessible format can be challenging, and researchers need to give attention to the language and format that they use. Particular care is required when research involves those who may not have the capacity to consent to research activity.

- *Harm and distress:* Some social research relates to sensitive and distressing themes. Researchers are required to prevent causing unnecessary distress and provide appropriate supports should a participant need care, advice or assistance.

- *Confidentiality:* Participants should expect that they will not be identified in the study and the findings will be provided in the form of an anonymous summary.

The majority of published research will have ethical permission from the relevant agency and having undergone this scrutiny provides some evidence of ethical standards. However, when appraising a survey the reader may also wish to consider additional factors that have ethical implications. The research project should be developed in collaboration with the relevant stakeholders, including service users and/or practitioners. It should be valuable to practice and necessary in producing evidence that does not already exist.

Research has the potential to benefit individuals and groups and, for that reason, the opportunity to participate should be provided fairly. There is a danger that some groups can be over-researched while others are unfairly excluded. Hayes and Devaney (2004) argue that research governance has the potential to limit the opportunity that specific groups have to benefit from participation in good quality research.

Method for data collection

A potential weakness of the survey method that an appraisal should consider is inconsistency related to the need for interpretation in the question-and-answer process. The challenge for the researcher is to reduce the potential for variation and ensure that the data gathered is an accurate measure of the issue under investigation. There is a range of techniques to ensure the tool used for data collection is an accurate (valid) and consistent (reliable) measure (see Table 5.3).

Table 5.3 Dimensions of validity and reliability

Survey validity

Face validity: In general, do questions measure what they are supposed to measure – e.g. does a panel of experts agree that this is a useful measure?

Construct validity: Do the questions measure the chosen theoretical concept – e.g. is the tool measuring parental stress as opposed to depression or anxiety?

Content validity: Do the questions include every single element of the concept – e.g. are all aspects of parental stress included?

Criterion validity: Does the measurement of the instrument correspond to another 'gold standard' measure – e.g. do the questions provide the same results as other validated measures?

Survey reliability

Test-retest reliability: Does the instrument provide consistent measures when repeated in identical circumstances? – e.g. does an IQ test provide the same result on the same child?

Inter-rater reliability: Do different interviewers using the same questions produce similar results?

Internal consistency: Do all of the questions relating to a theme provide consistent scores? – e.g. do the ten questions measuring parental stress correlate with each other?

The subject of maximising validity in survey design is discussed elsewhere (Bostwick and Kyle, 2011) but any appraisal of a survey method should establish the extent to which the design has included the following.

1. *Clear and explicit questions.* The research participant needs to understand exactly what is being asked of them and, if provided, the possible answers should cover all potential responses. The survey tool or interview should provide the necessary information and direction to promote ease of completion. Terms that are vague or that could have more than one meaning should be avoided or clarified.

2. *Objective and subjective measures.* Some data can be gathered using subjective measures.

3. *The use of scales.* Rating scales are valuable in surveys as they gather qualitative data in a quantitative manner adding depth and meaning to the survey approach. The scale provides a spectrum rather than a number of defined responses.

4. *Validated tools.* In survey research it is possible to use or incorporate a tool that has been previously validated. This provides confidence as long as the tool is used in the same context and manner as it was designed for. Validated tools now exist for many aspects of human life and behaviours such as quality of life, parental stress and mental well-being.

5. *Piloting.* Having designed a series of questions it is useful to test them with a small group of respondents similar to the focus population – i.e. individuals not included in the sample. Piloting assesses the ease with which participants complete the survey and identifies any potential areas of confusion or mistakes.

Research Example

Promoting validity in a survey

In a survey of students' perceptions of practice learning opportunities, the self-completed questionnaire included the following.

- *Objective measures*: on average, how long did supervision last?
- *Rating scales*: state overall satisfaction with practice teaching between 1 and 7.
- *Validated tool*: supervision styles inventory (Friedlander and Ward, 1984).
- *Piloting*: the questionnaire was piloted with five students who were not participating in the actual survey.

(Killick, 2005)

While all the above safeguards relate to most forms of survey research, special consideration needs to be given to the human factors inherent in the interview process. This is further complicated if there are a number of different interviewers involved in the study. Interviewers can be trained to reduce the bias that they introduce to the process. Steps can also be taken to ensure that each interview is conducted in an identical manner. There should be clear guidelines to the way in which questions are worded and responses recorded.

Analysing data

We have seen how the validity and reliability of a survey are affected by the way in which questions are asked and answered. In a similar way, the approach to analysing the data has the potential to improve or erode the accuracy of the final results. Data analysis involves the restructuring of the available information and it therefore needs to be carefully, systematically undertaken and explicitly described. The approach to analysis should flow logically from the research question and the type of data that is being collected. Statistical procedures can be used:

- to describe frequencies and distributions;

- to measure the impact of independent variables – e.g. age on dependent variables or health status; or

- to test a set as part of the research question.

When used correctly, statistical analysis can describe data and explore patterns within it. Sadly, the manipulation of data can also be deliberately or inadvertently misused causing misinterpretation and incorrect conclusions. When appraising a survey report special attention should be given to the way in which the data has been analysed. This is not easy, as the average social worker is not always proficient in statistics. Good research reports are often able to describe the process used for analysis in terms that practitioners and even lay people could understand, but it is helpful to have a grasp of the basic statistical concepts. Equally, it is useful to understand dubious techniques and ways in which data can be misrepresented.

The data set is cleaned to check for errors and missing data. At this stage an initial stage analysis will provide basis information about the data that has been gathered. It is possible to check if there are any pre-existing patterns in the data that might confuse further analysis. It is expected that the independent variables will be exactly that – independent of each other (uncorrelated or orthogonal). Computer software is used to provide a descriptive summary of each variable allowing the prevalence and distribution of each variable for this sample to be discussed. The most commonly used descriptive measures are shown in Table 5.4. It should be noted that specific measures are required for different types of variables. It is not possible to calculate a mean of the variable age even if it has been coded with numeric values.

Table 5.4   Quantitative terminology

Frequency	The number of times each value has occurred
Percentage	The frequency as a percentage of the total
Range	The lowest and highest value provided
Mean	The average value
Mode	The most frequent value
Median	The middle value

Research findings

Quantitative data can be presented in the form of **descriptive statistics** that describe the sample using summaries of each of the measured characteristics and **inferential statistics** that make predictions about the entire populations.

Descriptive statistics are presented as frequency tables and measures of central tendency like the mean value. An example would be the numbers of a sample who worked in children's services or the average age of the sample. Often percentage values are helpful in comparing results but the frequency must always be included to give meaning to the result. Similarly, it is sometimes helpful to illustrate findings using a histogram or chart but these should be accompanied by the numerical data to allow further scrutiny.

Inferential statistics use techniques to investigate relationships and estimate how likely these are to occur in the broader population. An example would be to calculate if the average age of social workers was different in each programme of care and if this difference could be said to be statistically significant. There is a range of measures that will calculate the strength of a relationship in a representative sample and the probability that the relationship can be said to exist within the wider population. Tests for **significance** are discussed at length elsewhere (De Vaus, 2013; Pallant, 2013) and each test has specific uses and assumptions. To appraise the statistical findings the reader should be able to identify test value and the probability value. The smaller the probability value (p-value) the more likely that the noticed difference is due to a relationship and not coincidence. A small p-value (typically ≤ 0.05) indicates a significant result suggesting that there is a relationship in the total population.

Research Example

Strength of relationship

An analysis of social worker age and programme of care using the test ANOVA provided the following result [$f\,(9,2245) = 1.961$ $p = 0.04$]. The f-value of 1.961 shows the strength of the relationship and the p-value shows the probability that the sample estimate relates to the total population.

A good research report will endeavour to present the findings in a manner that is clear and understandable to the average practitioner. This may involve an explanation of the tests used, the meaning of the numbers and any possible concerns or limitations. In particular the report should be honest when low response rates or small numbers in subcategories may impact on the reliability of the outcome. While a survey of 300 social workers looks robust the analysis may be looking specifically at managers, who form a smaller subgroup. If it turns out that only 12 managers replied we need to be careful in how we analyse the information from this small group.

The report should make reference to all data gathered and explain any omissions. It is possible that work limits may not allow a full discussion of the data gathered or some results may not relate to the research question being discussed. However, the reader should be alert to the selective presentation of data. It is possible that an author could focus on those results that best support the argument being made while skimming over the less supportive data. As discussed earlier in this chapter, a key issue for survey quality is the number of non-respondents and the make-up of this group. A good report will explicitly state the return rate and any impact that this might have on the reading of findings. Often there is a section in the report where methodological and practical limitations are discussed. This should be given special attention when critically appraising the study.

The final section in a survey report is often the discussion section where key findings are identified and comparisons are made to other published studies. While findings are factual and objective, the discussion allows for some interpretation and application. In some cases recommendations are also made but it is important that the author does not overstate their case or go beyond the scope of the findings. It is tempting to 'spin' research results to support an argument or justify an intervention, but a good discussion will present the range of possible meanings and allow the reader to come to their own conclusions. Research findings are rarely black and white, and it is the responsibility of the author to outline the most robust findings and point out where interaction effects or confounding factors may have muddied the waters.

Generalisability

In appraising a survey report, the reader needs to consider how relevant the material is to their setting and location. It is unlikely that the study was conducted in an identical time, location and client group. It is dangerous to presume that a study conducted in Boston will be relevant to Belfast or an intervention with people who have mental health difficulties can be translated to adults with learning disabilities. The reader must compare the contexts and the populations before presuming that the findings can be generalised. Ultimately, the only way to be sure is to undertake a separate research study.

Becoming a social worker

It is important that a social worker is able to appraise research evidence provided from survey methods whether they seek to describe the characteristics of a group or investigate the relationship between two or more variables.

Reflection Point

- How does quantitative survey data inform your practice and that of your team?

Activity 5.1

Evidence into practice task

- Search a database to identify a paper reporting a study that asked a question about the perceptions of the recipients of a social work intervention and which used qualitative research methods.
- Having identified a paper reporting a study that used a survey method, use the appraisal tool QAT-S: Quality Appraisal Tool: Surveys in Appendix 1 to extract key information about the methods used and to learn to appraise the quality of a survey.

Chapter Summary

- The use of the survey method to gather quantitative data is explained.
- The survey method involves a question, rational, method analysis and findings.
- The overall quality of a report is only as good as the weakest part of the process.
- The quality indicators of the appraisal tool QAT-S: Quality Appraisal Tool: Surveys in Appendix 1 are explained.

Further Reading

Aldridge, A and Levine, K (2001) *Surveying the Social World: Principles and practice in survey research.* Buckingham: Open University Press.

This text provides an overview of survey research and is particularly helpful in its description of question design and data collection.

De Vaus, D (2013) *Surveys in Social Research* (6th edition). London: Routledge.

Now in its 6th edition, this book outlines the key components of a quality survey design.

McColl, E, Jacoby, A, Thomas, L, Scoutter, J, Bamford, C, Steen, N, Thomas, R, Harvey, E, Garratt, A and Bond, J (2001) Design and use of questionnaires: A review of best practice applicable to surveys of health service staff and patients. *Health Technology Assessment 2001,* 5 (31). Available at: www.journalslibrary.nihr.ac.uk/__data/assets/pdf_file/ooo/64833/FullReport-hta5310.pdf

This resource is written for healthcare but is equally applicable to social work and social care.

Chapter 6

Appraising qualitative studies

Introduction

This chapter focuses on appraising rigour in qualitative research. It begins by outlining the essential purpose of qualitative research, accessing real-world experiences through data-rich respondents. The core method of most qualitative research – thematic analysis – is described and a brief outline provided on major qualitative research methods, as an essential preliminary to appraising the quality of qualitative research. Major approaches to appraising qualitative research are outlined prior to considering in turn the ten quality appraisal questions as outlined in the QAT-Q: Quality Appraisal Tool: Qualitative studies in Appendix 2. Some more general discussion of the appraisal of research quality that is relevant to qualitative studies can be found in Chapter 5.

The heart of qualitative research: thematic analysis

Qualitative research is appropriate to explore meanings, perceptions and constructs in real-world contexts where there is limited previous research on the topic. The focus is on language, meanings, perspectives and social (including both life and work) processes as experienced by those from whom data is gathered. Qualitative research is not suited to testing a theory in the way this phrase is understood in quantitative research, although one qualitative method – **interpretative phenomenological analysis (IPA)** (see box below) – is suited to 'testing out' a theory in a different context. The best qualitative research builds a theory, a model or a new understanding or conceptualisation of the topic of interest. Qualitative research is not suited to measuring or comparing effects or causes, although it may provide insight into people's perceptions of these. Within another qualitative method – grounded theory (see box below) – the process of qualitative research is described as 'analytic induction' or 'grounded creativity'. The researcher is aiming to draw out the essential meanings or sense that people make of their experiences and their cognitive processes in understanding the identified aspect of their world.

An essential dimension of qualitative research is to capture data from an 'insider' perspective. Enabling research participants to speak openly and honestly about their experiences is essential to good qualitative research. This will clearly be more challenging on some topics than others. A survey might be used to measure people's attitudes to something, but will be a clumsy instrument if the wording of the questions is not appropriate to the constructs and language of respondents. A qualitative study sacrifices the representativeness of a large sample, such as might be used in a survey, for an in-depth and more nuanced understanding from a smaller sample of people. The aim is to create a new theoretical understanding or model that is true to 'typical' experiences of respondents, not to measure representativeness of predefined constructs among a population.

Core methods of qualitative research

The focus of all qualitative research is the natural settings in which people live and work, help and are helped. Qualitative research aims to capture something of the richness and complexity of people's lived experience. There are various approaches to qualitative research, just as there is a variety of methods of statistical analysis with quantitative data. It is impossible in this short text, and inappropriate to our target readership, to attempt to explain in detail these various approaches. A brief summary with references is provided in the Research Summary box and a valuable comparison is provided in Starks and Trinidad (2007). For the present purpose we expect readers to gain a clear understanding of when qualitative methods in general are appropriate (as opposed to experimental or survey methods), and what they can and cannot be expected to achieve. Understanding the particular attributes of different qualitative methods is something that would be expected at Ph.D. level, but not within qualifying or post-qualifying social work studies per se. This chapter focuses on the essentials of qualitative methods and their appraisal.

Research Summary

Some major qualitative research approaches

Discourse analysis

The focus is on use of language – written, spoken or signed – in its social context of language. The method aims to understand the 'social rules' for the discourse and hence the meaning of interactions and dominant ideas in a social group (Gee, 2005).

Ethnography

The focus is on how people understand their social world through immersion of the researcher in the milieu so as to gain valid participant-researcher observations. Issues of gaining entry and acceptance are often central, as are issues of interpreting the culture and social norms (Fetterman, 1998) and identifying and describing shared meanings.

> **Grounded theory**
>
> Grounded theory aims to understand people's experiences and use this to create an original theoretical understanding, without imposing any theoretical model on the data gathering or analysis. It emphasises the helpful concept of **saturation sampling** (see below in relation to sampling), 'constant comparison' of data with what has already been gathered, and the development of an insightful conceptualisation of the social world drawn from the meanings attributed by participants (Strauss and Corbin, 1998).
>
> **Interpretative phenomenological analysis (IPA)**
>
> IPA is designed to give insights into how a person, in a given context, makes sense of a phenomenon. This usually relates to an important life event or relationship, such as illness, life transitions and distress. IPA can also be used if you have a basic theory and want to refine it or 'test it out' in a new context (J.A. Smith et al., 2009).

Some qualitative methods such as ethnography move the balance more towards observation, rather than relying exclusively on the analysis of words. Other methods such as discourse analysis may include oral, written and other forms of recorded narrative as data within one cohesive analysis. Nonetheless, an understanding of underlying meanings, as in basic thematic analysis, underpins these qualitative approaches also. A 'blank box' following a prompt within a survey, such as are found in many service evaluations and professional audits, gathers qualitative data. However, the lack of interaction to prompt and explore perceptions and experiences will limit the richness of data available for analysis compared to qualitative research as the word is used by qualitative researchers (Taylor, 2016). Such qualitative data gathered from surveys can enrich the presentation of quantitative data, but is not suited to developing a coherent understanding of participants' experiences.

Major approaches to appraising qualitative research

Four basic approaches to appraising the quality of qualitative research may be identified.

1. Use criteria specific to that particular qualitative method only.

2. Use completely different criteria from those used to appraise quantitative studies.

3. Use criteria for quantitative studies with additional criteria specific to qualitative studies.

4. Use the same criteria as in appraising quantitative studies, but applied differently.

The use of criteria specific to that particular qualitative method, as in (1), has the advantage of fine-tuning the appraisal to the specific methodology. This is perhaps more important for a method such as **ethnography**, which has some features that are distinct from many other qualitative methods. The use of completely different criteria from those used for appraising quantitative studies, as in (2), suggests that the appraiser does not perceive commonalities between criteria for qualitative and quantitative methods. The use of some criteria that are the same as for quantitative studies but with further criteria that only apply to qualitative studies, as in (3), is more common (e.g. Elliot et al., 1999). The approach in this book is within the fourth category above, using the same ten broad criteria for all types of studies but applying these as appropriate to the three main types of methodology discussed here.

Rationale for the study

The first question to ask is whether the rationale for the study is clear. The essence of qualitative research methods is to create a conceptualisation of the lived reality for respondents. The focus is on the experiences of respondents, and the meanings that they ascribe to events and their perceptions of these. Qualitative research is seeking an understanding that is generalisable in terms of being useful for understanding in a general sense of what is typically happening for people in this situation.

An essential point to grasp in appraising qualitative research is that it is suitable for addressing different types of questions from those suited to being addressed by survey or (quasi-)experimental studies. Many of the heated debates about 'evidence-based practice' seem to get lost in the misunderstanding that the only question worth asking is about measuring effectiveness. The appraisal of study designs appropriate to asking that question are discussed in Chapter 7. Our focus in this chapter is on questions about experiences and perceptions. There are many useful questions to be asked about people's experiences of receiving and providing interventions that can usefully inform the development and provision of interventions.

Essential design and purpose

The rationale for qualitative research is that there is a topic that requires exploration. Any research is to create an original, generalisable understanding that fills a gap in human knowledge. However, the primary justification for qualitative research is that the experience or situation is so unclear or ill-defined that we do not have concepts to describe and discuss it. Once we have a model, a theory or concepts, a quantitative method can be used to measure the concept or to count the prevalence of the construct within some group of people.

Sampling

A good qualitative study should identify the sample of people from whom the data is drawn in terms of relevant characteristics. This helps the reader to 'situate the sample' and thereby appraise methodological issues as well as generalisability to his or her own setting. What characteristics are deemed 'relevant' will, of course, depend on the topic of the study. If it is a study of clients, the socio-demographic data gathered might be a classification of the type of problem that brought them to a social worker, which services they have received, age-band, family composition, etc. If it is a study of social workers, for example, the socio-demographic data gathered might include years qualified, years in this type of work, years in this particular team or unit, etc.

Research Example

Identifying characteristics of study participants

Staff	Employer				Sex		Years in this work	
	1	2	3	4	M	F		
Consultant geriatrician	1	1	1	1	2	2	11	17
General medical practitioner	1	1	1	1	4	0	10	25
Social worker	5	7	4	2	7	11	1	14
Other care manager	1	1	4	5	1	10	1	15
Community nurse	5	8	2	4	1	18	1	25
Occupational therapist	5	3	4	8	0	20	3	24
Home care manager	0	6	3	2	1	10	1	18
Hospital discharge team	3	4	4	1	1	11	1	13
Total	21	31	23	24	17	82	–	–

(Taylor and Donnelly, 2006b, p243)

The primary requirement of a sample for a qualitative study is that respondents are 'information-rich'. They need to have had experiences relevant to the focus of the study. This is often referred to as a **purposive sample**. Thus, clients might be asked about experiences of needs or journeys through services or through an informal process that has brought some healing or resolution of issues, etc. Staff might be asked about their experiences of providing services or some aspect of this such as stressful aspects, or aspects that give greatest job satisfaction or experiences of fear, etc. Qualitative studies generally become weaker when participants are asked about hypothetical situations which are further removed from their own experience.

A key skill in qualitative research is for the researcher to reflect continuously on the data gathered, comparing new material with what has been gathered already. The data is analysed in terms of themes or topics. As the number of interviews or focus groups conducted increases, gradually the number of new themes emerging slows down. New respondents say things that reinforce what previous respondents have said, but the number of new insights or conceptualisations reduces. Eventually, one would expect that on the core topic of the qualitative study a stage would be reached where no new themes come from further interviews or focus group sessions. This is known as 'saturation', a concept drawn from grounded theory (Strauss and Corbin, 1998). It is a rational way to define a 'sufficient' sample for qualitative research in terms of being able to justify the theoretical model derived from the study. 'Sampling to saturation' would be an indicator of strength in a qualitative study.

Ethical aspects

Ethical issues for qualitative research relate particularly to (1) the face-to-face nature of data gathering, and (2) the inherent 'subjectivity' of qualitative research. In terms of the face-to-face contact through interviews or focus groups, one should consider whether and what relationship exists between the researcher and participants. How do they relate to each other in terms of roles in relation to the focus of the study? How might participants perceive the researcher?

Research Summary

Perceived role and status of researcher

Background: *Qualitative research methods are now recognized as valuable tools for primary care. With the increasing emphasis on evidence-based medicine and critical appraisal of published work, it is important that qualitative researchers are transparent about their methods and discuss the impact of the research process on their data.*

Objectives: *To consider the impact of the professional background of researchers on in-depth interviewing in primary care.*

Methods: *We compare interactions between the interviewer and respondents in two qualitative interview studies of heart disease. Both samples consisted of 60 middle-aged men and women from a range of social backgrounds living in the West of Scotland. One study was conducted by a GP and the other by a sociologist.*

Results: *Some interview interactions were common to both researchers; for example, interviews were often regarded by respondents as therapeutic. However, some interactions seemed to be related to the researcher's professional background. The GP's perceived higher status led to obscuring of her personal characteristics. The sociologist was often perceived as a 'young woman' rather than defined by her professional role. Thus, respondents' perceptions of the interviewer influenced the interview interactions.*

Conclusions: *Appraising qualitative research depends on the transparency with which the research process is described. Awareness of professional background is particularly important for university departments of primary care (which often include doctors, nurses and social scientists), and should be considered carefully in designing, carrying out and disseminating the results of qualitative studies.*

(Richards and Emslie, 2000)

The researcher gathering rich qualitative data needs to interact with the people who are the source of data. This is an essential part of the process. There is, of course, the possibility of bias due to preconceived ideas of the researcher or the perceptions of the respondents about the researcher. Respondents may be inclined to say what they think the researcher wants to hear, depending on the perceived role, affiliation or status of the researcher. (Note that this is not unique to qualitative methods; similar biases can occur with surveys.) There is the possibility of bias from the researcher in the analysis, and in the frame of reference or knowledge base that is used.

An important dimension of qualitative research to address this subjectivity is to ensure that there is a reflective process built into the study. Quite apart from the emphasis within the social work profession on reflection as a key aspect of learning to apply theory to practice, qualitative research emphasises reflexivity as a research process. It is important that the researcher reflects on his or her own role, assumptions and frame of reference. An awareness of how he or she might be perceived can enable the researcher to address this during the interviews or focus groups, as well as enabling greater objectivity during analysis. Reflexivity is regarded as an essential component of good qualitative research.

The ideal for good social work research is to engage key stakeholders at each stage of the process, to ensure that there will be value not just for the researcher but also for managers and practitioners as well as clients and families. Engaging clients as co-researchers can be regarded as a laudable ethical principle, and is particularly relevant to qualitative research. The public, or users of research or users of services are increasingly having a role in shaping research priorities, in gathering data as peer-researchers and assisting in data analysis. This may give valuable insights into the meaning intended by respondents (e.g. Taylor et al., 2014). The engagement of peer-researchers needs careful planning and carries inherent risks as well as benefits. The materials developed by the INVOLVE organisation, noted in the Further Reading section of Chapter 1, are a valuable resource.

Research Summary

Example of involving peer-researchers

This qualitative study used data from eight focus groups involving 58 people aged over 65 years in both urban and rural settings across Northern Ireland and the Republic of Ireland. Following training, four older people assisted in facilitation and analysis as peer-researchers. Increasing lack of respect within society was experienced as abusive. The vulnerability of older people to abuse was perceived as relating to the need for help and support, where standing up for themselves might have repercussions for the person's health or safety. Emotional abusiveness was viewed as underpinning all forms of abuse,

> *and as influencing its experienced severity. Respondents' views as to whether an action was abusive required an understanding of intent: some actions that professionals might view as abusive were regarded as acceptable if they were in the older person's best interests. Preventing abuse requires a wide-ranging approach including rebuilding respect for older people within society. Procedures to prevent elder abuse need to take into account the emotional impact of family relationships and intent, not just a description of behaviors that have occurred. The involvement of peer-researchers contributed to the empathy with the social world in which respondents had grown up, and the social changes that they had experienced during their lifetime.*
>
> (Taylor et al., 2014)

As with all research, appropriate ethical approval is essential and should be recorded in the paper reporting the study. Usually this reporting is quite brief, and a reader expecting a full discussion of ethical issues is likely to be disappointed. This brevity is largely attributable to (1) the pressure on word length in the publication, and (2) a fairly reasonable assumption that in 'developed' democratic countries reasonably similar standards of consent, confidentiality and conflict of interest pertain, and are regulated through comparable ethical approval structures. Ethical approval for research was traditionally provided by universities as a peer-review process. However, increasingly for health and social care, governments are taking a stronger lead in oversight of ethical issues to ensure a more transparent accountability to society.

Data collection

As with surveys (Chapter 5) and experimental studies (Chapter 7), the quality of the data-gathering tools will influence quality. A qualitative study should make the method of data collection clear. Most often it will be focus groups or interviews. Has the number and length of these been indicated in the paper? Did participants take part in just one session each or more than one? What degree of structure was provided for the sessions? Many studies describe themselves as using 'semi-structured interviews', which means that there are prompts to guide the discussion but substantial latitude for participants to say what is in their hearts. A better study will have a clear and justifiable rationale for the choice between group and individual methods of data gathering. Issues of concern might relate to such as:

- ease of discussing this topic in a group setting in terms of embarrassment;

- time constraint in terms of conducting a large number of interviews; or

- timing of group sessions in terms of people being available at that particular time – for example, if staff are particularly busy or do shift-work, or have to provide 'cover' for care or availability to deal with callers or telephone calls.

Ethnographic studies make extensive use of observation as a data-gathering method. This is more susceptible to criticism of researcher bias. The essence of the method is not to use a pre-formulated classification to observe behaviours, but to study the people in their natural environment without preconceived conceptualisations to best understand their perceptions on their world. Reflexivity as discussed above is crucial in such observational studies.

Diaries are being used increasingly as a data-gathering tool for qualitative research. They have the strength of recording more contemporaneously with the events taking place than recounting to an interviewer at a later date. However, they can suffer from a weakness in not permitting the research to explore and discuss the issues. One way to enrich diary studies is to conduct a number of interviews at intervals with participants where their diary entries are discussed. Other things being equal, this has clear strengths of both contemporaneity and interaction as a data-gathering method.

Research Summary

Using a range of data-gathering tools

This qualitative study focused on the identity transition of women to motherhood. Twenty items of data were gathered from each of four women, including diary entries, interviews, observation and completion of a repertory grid. A major finding was that the changing relationship of self to others is facilitated during pregnancy in social occasions. Pregnancy provides an opportunity for a woman to invoke her future mother-self.

(Smith, 1999)

Analysis of data

All qualitative methods are essentially about understanding people's words and behaviours, rather than measuring or counting something as in quantitative methods. The essence of this process of analysis is generally known as **thematic analysis**. As the transcripts of the interviews or focus groups are analysed, the main themes in what people are saying are identified. In particular, the utterances with common meanings are grouped together, even if the wording is different. The researcher will continuously reflect on the data, becoming immersed in it so as to identify commonalities across people's experiences. The themes being identified are compared with each other so as to reorganise data between themes and to refashion the themes as appropriate. This process of assigning meaning to data is often called 'coding' the data. Analysis of qualitative data is about the representation of social phenomena, such as needs and care processes. The qualitative research creates an account of these social processes, and thereby constructs a version of the social work and social actor observed (Coffey and Atkinson, 1998).

Research Example

Deriving themes from codes

With the increasing pressure on social and healthcare resources, professionals have to be more explicit in their decision making regarding the long-term care of older people. This grounded theory study used 19 focus groups and 9 semi-structured interviews (99 staff in total) to explore professional perspectives on this decision making. Focus group participants and interviewees comprised care managers, social workers, consultant geriatricians, general medical practitioners, community nurses, home care managers, occupational therapists and hospital discharge support staff. Analysis of paragraphs from transcripts gave codes such as:

- *knowing someone who was burgled;*
- *loss of respect from local youth;*
- *concern at local crime rate;*
- *assault would be devastating!;*
- *refusing a service (stair rail at the front door).*

These codes begin to develop into a theme: fear of burglary and assault. Other themes also emerged from the data, including:

- *fear of burglary and assault;*
- *fear of falling;*
- *measures of physical needs do not equate to 'need' for admission to care home;*
- *admission often arises in a crisis, such as returning home from hospital.*

These themes formed the element of a model conceptualising admission to long-term care as occurring when either:

- *the older person living alone no longer has confidence to continue doing so; OR*
- *family members can no longer cope with the care they have been providing.*

The emerging themes spanned context, clients, families and services. Decisions were often prompted by a crisis, hindering professionals seeking to make a measured assessment. Fear of burglary and assault, and the willingness and availability of family to help were major factors in decisions about living at home. Service availability in terms of public funding for community care, the availability of home care workers and workload pressures on primary care services influenced decision 'thresholds' regarding admission to institutional care. Assessment tools designed to assist decision making about the long-term care of older people need to take into account the critical aspects of individual fears and motivation, family support and the availability of publicly funded services as well as functional and medical needs.

(Taylor and Donnelly, 2006a)

Statement of findings

The findings of the study should be clearly presented and in an intelligible way. Making sense and 'ringing true' are signs of good qualitative research. All major themes should be substantiated with direct quotations or observations, so that readers can appraise for themselves the relationship between the data and the analysis.

A good qualitative study aims to create a new theoretical or conceptual understanding of the experiences or conceptualisations of some group of people. It is not a statistical model, but rather a theoretical model which aims to be useful in providing a working understanding of what typically happens in these types of situations or processes. Often what is achieved is a range of themes that illustrate the topic, as opposed to demonstrating typical mechanisms or processes.

Research Summary

Creating a qualitative model

Risk management systems and structures are developing rapidly within UK health and personal social services. However, the risk management strategies of organisations need to take into account the conceptual frameworks used by professionals. This grounded theory study used data from 19 focus groups and 9 semi-structured interviews (99 staff in total) to explore perspectives on risk and decision-making regarding the long-term care of older people. Focus group participants and interviewees comprised social workers, care managers, consultant geriatricians, general medical practitioners, community nurses, occupational therapists, home care managers and hospital discharge support staff. Social work and healthcare professionals conceptualised risk and its management according to six paradigms that appeared to be in a state of reciprocal tension: (1) Identifying and Meeting Needs, (2) Minimising Situational Hazards, (3) Protecting this Individual and Others, (4) Balancing Benefits and Harms, (5) Accounting for Resources and Priorities, and (6) Wariness of Lurking Conflicts. Each conceptualisation of risk had its sphere of relevance and inconsistencies at the boundaries of this. Professionals seemed to use the conceptualisation that was most appropriate for the immediate situation, changing to another conceptualisation when this was more useful. The effective translation into practice of risk-management strategies needs to address the complex and often contradictory issues facing health and social services professionals.

(Taylor, 2006b)

A good theory or model has a clear focus, and is coherent and useful in understanding some aspect of social life. The model will illustrate how these types of individuals typically perceive, understand, rationalise or make meaning out of their experiences. Each of the elements is supported by study data, with no gaping gaps. A robust theory will stand the test of time, but will also be modifiable (see Charmaz, 2006). A theory derived from qualitative research provides a way of understanding typical social mechanisms and processes.

Credibility of findings

A key question to ask about a qualitative study is about the confidence that the reader can have that the words attributed to respondents were actually spoken by them. In general nowadays one would expect data to be recorded with an electronic digital recorder and in previous times on a tape recorder. There should be some sort of audit trail visible such that the person supervising the research can be a 'guarantor' that the front-line researcher is not making up the data. In order to demonstrate that the analysis is based on a wide range of respondents, it is customary to provide some ascription against each quotation used. These ascriptions might indicate the sex, age, job role or service need, etc. as appropriate to the focus of the study. Clearly, the researchers should also ensure that the detail does not breach confidentiality. For focus group discussions, each group should be given a descriptor such as geographical location or profession or labelled A, B, C, etc.

An important methodological feature that can add to quality of qualitative research is where the main researcher's coding is 'verified' through a process involving one or more other researchers. A typical process is where a second person codes some or all transcripts. This might be a person consciously chosen as being familiar with the topic area but from a different professional discipline. It is not necessary for the 'second coder' to code every transcript. Often the second coder will code every second or every third transcript. Another approach is to have the second coder involved more frequently in analysing the earlier transcripts (when the themes are changing more rapidly) and at longer intervals between later transcripts (Taylor, 2006b). Peer-researchers may also be involved in analysis to reduce the bias of having only one person coding data (Begley et al., 2012).

Research Summary

Dual coding

Care at home is fundamental to community care policy, but the simultaneous growth of health and safety regulation has implications for home care services because of the duty of employers towards home care workers. This grounded theory study used 19 focus groups and 9 semi-structured interviews (99 staff in total) to explore professional perspectives on risk and decision making in relation to the care of older people. Focus group participants and interviewees comprised care managers, social workers, consultant geriatricians, general medical practitioners, community nurses, home care managers, occupational therapists and hospital discharge support staff. Two researchers coded a selection of tapes independently to give greater validity to the development of themes, developing an 'operational definition' of each code so as to aid clarity of language and consistency of coding. The initial plan was that the second researcher would code tapes numbered 1, 2, 4, 8, 16 etc. of the chronological sequence,

> *so as to give a smaller interval in the earlier stages when the codes were developing more quickly. The sequence of this 'ideal model' was modified slightly so that the second coder would also sample the range of professions and organisations within which they worked. We sought inter-coder agreement at a certain level of the coding structure (two headings down), thus providing a certain level of 'fault tolerance'. The coders generally reached an agreement level of approximately 80%. Home care workers faced a wide range of hazards in the homes of clients, who themselves were faced with adapting their living habits due to their changing health and care needs and 'risks.' Creative approaches were used to ensure the health and safety of home care workers and simultaneously to meet the choices of clients. Staff experienced feelings of conflict when they judged it necessary to impose their way of providing home care and thus impose their values on clients to create a safe working environment. There was variation between and within organisations in terms of the staff focus on client needs or on their employer responsibility towards home care workers. The planning of home care services must take account of both the choices of clients and the hazards facing home care staff.*
>
> (Taylor and Donnelly, 2006b)

Computer software can improve the quality of qualitative analysis by reducing the effects of fatigue, and by making large data sets more manageable. Creating a visual 'tree' of codes is perhaps one of the most useful features of qualitative data analysis software, and can lead to a greater richness of analysis through the ready visualisation of a large amount of data.

The questions that we might ask in terms of qualitative research include the following.

- Did the sampling frame contain known bias?

- Was the questioning and context effective for participants to express their views?

- Do the themes reflect the meanings of participants as in the quotes provided?

- Is there sufficient internal evidence for the explanatory accounts developed?

- Are findings true to the data and do they allow the reader to see the analysis used?

A number of other approaches may be used in qualitative research to enhance rigour. **Respondent validation** is where participants in the study are provided with feedback on findings and asked to comment on them. This might be with individuals or groups, and might be in relation to their own responses or the responses to the overall studies. A common approach is to invite individuals who have participated in focus groups or individual interviews to attend a session where the findings of the whole study are presented.

Research Summary

Respondent validation

The experience of people living as a minority in Northern Ireland during the period after the worst of the civil violence is of interest in understanding their feelings and their perceptions of the issues; and in exploring possibilities for further community integration. The study entailed twenty interviews with individuals or couples from each of the two main parts of the community who were living as a minority within a locality where they were not the dominant ethnic (political) group. Each interview was recorded by hand by a note-taker working alongside the interviewer. After the interview process, participants were sent a summary of about three pages of their own responses and were invited to comment on this. One married couple who participated in this process reported that commenting on the transcript enabled them to correct the interpretation of one of the (approximately ten) main points that they had made and also to add a point which they had forgotten to make at the time.

Expert validation refers to using the opinions of people who have an expertise in the field, but who have not participated in the study, to comment on the study findings. This may be professionals working in the field or people who are 'experts by experience' but who are not respondents in this study. As with *participant validation*, the essential question being addressed is the extent to which the findings ring true to their knowledge and experience.

For qualitative research and the types of research questions it is suited to address, the focus in terms of credibility is in reflecting the nature of the phenomenon or ideas under study as perceived by respondents with experience living or working (or receiving or giving services) in that field. **Validity** is a central concept in terms of credibility just as with surveys and experimental studies. However, *the inference that can be drawn from qualitative data concerns the nature of the phenomenon being studied but not its prevalence or statistical distribution* (see surveys: Ritchie and Lewis, 2003, p277). This also contrasts with experimental studies where the essence of validity concerns the elimination of other causal factors (see Chapter 7).

Another key concept in terms of credibility is reliability, as with the other types of research design discussed in this book. Is enough information provided for the study to be replicated? Such openness about methods provides opportunity for others to challenge findings and to seek to confirm whether there are similar findings in other contexts.

Quality of discussion and conclusions

It is important that the conclusions of the study are justified by the findings presented. It can be very tempting for enthusiastic researchers to get carried away by their own ideas and present these as if they are substantiated. A study has added credibility if its findings are triangulated with other studies. In the discussion section, all papers should discuss the extent to which the findings confirm or contradict previous studies in the field. In the case of qualitative research, a particular priority will be to locate the study in terms of other theoretical frameworks and to explain the niche that is filled by this study. The new conceptualisation created should be connected with other theory and conclusions drawn as to how this creates a fuller theoretical model or, conversely, how it highlights an apparent contradiction which needs to be resolved through further research.

This process of locating the study findings in relation to other studies essentially involves using existing theory. It is an important quality criterion that the paper explains clearly which material is a finding from this study and what is drawn from other research. It is important that existing theory sensitises rather than blinkers the analysis. A researcher cannot begin with a 'tabula rasa' (blank slate), and needs to have prepared for the study through understanding the existing literature. However, it is important that this knowledge is used to enable a more sensitive data-gathering process and a more insightful analysis, rather than forcing the study into an existing theoretical framework (Coffey and Atkinson, 1998).

Research Summary

Model derived from qualitative research

1. STEP 1 *Resolving to stop.*
2. STEP 2 *Breaking away from addiction.*
3. STEP 3 *Staying abstinent.*
4. STEP 4 *Becoming and being ordinary.*

Themes within Step 4: Becoming and being ordinary:

a. *Identity transformation.*
b. *Emergent identity – reverting to unspoilt identity – extending identity.*
c. *Surmounting the barriers to change.*
d. *Relationships with addicts, non-addicts – speech nuances.*
e. *Stabilisation of identity, perspective & relationships.*
f. *Social commitments – drug-related experiences that confirm identity change.*

(Recovery from heroin addiction; Biernacki, 1986)

Alternative explanations for the data should also be explored rather than ignored. This might be through comparison with previous research or theory. A good theory or model (conceptualisation) developed through a qualitative study should:

- have a clear focus;

- have elements that are supported by data;

- be useful;

- be coherent;

- have no gaping gaps;

- be durable over time;

- be modifiable; and

- have explanatory power.

(Adapted from Charmaz, 2006, p6)

Generalisability

The essence of qualitative research is to create an understanding of the 'world' from the perspective of some participants within that environment. An aspect of appraising a qualitative study will be the extent to which the participants studied might have experiences which aid an insight into the conceptualisations of the people who you wish to understand better. In appraising this aspect you will want to consider the features of the study participants and their environment which are similar to, and different from, the context for which you are considering its value.

Generalisability of qualitative research is not based on the statistical representativeness of the sample from which participants are drawn, as it would be for a survey. The basic principle is the same in terms of considering the extent to which the findings can be generalised beyond the sample studied. However, the key issue is whether the theoretical principles developed can be applied to a wider population. For more detailed discussion, the reader is referred to Ritchie and Lewis (2003) in the Further Reading section.

Becoming a social worker

Being able to appraise research that has used a qualitative method is a valuable skill for the professional social worker, not least because so many studies in social work use qualitative methods. It is important that professionals in the field are able to discern the quality of such papers and the extent to which they gather valid data to inform practice. This chapter relates particularly to domain 5.11 of the PCF on demonstrating an understanding of qualitative research methods.

Reflection Point

- How does this type of knowledge of clients' perceptions inform your practice?

Activity 6.1

Evidence into practice task

- Search a database to identify a paper reporting a study that asked a question about the perceptions of the recipients of a social work intervention and that used qualitative research methods.
- Having identified a paper reporting a study that used qualitative methods, use the appraisal tool QAT-Q: Quality Appraisal Tool: Qualitative studies in Appendix 2 to extract key information about the methods used and to learn to appraise the quality of a qualitative study.

Chapter Summary

- The essential principles of thematic analysis which underpin all qualitative research have been described.
- The main approaches to qualitative research are outlined so as to aid the reader's understanding of papers being appraised.
- The main approaches to appraising qualitative research are outlined, and the approach used here is located in that context.
- The ten points of the appraisal tool QAT-Q: Quality Appraisal Tool: Qualitative studies in Appendix 2 are outlined and explained.

Further Reading

Charmaz, K (2006) *Constructing Grounded Theory*. New York: SAGE.

This is a good textbook on grounded theory, but straightforward enough for application to general thematic analysis.

Corbin, J and Strauss, AL (2008) *Basics of Qualitative Research: Techniques and procedures for developing grounded theory* (3rd edition). Thousand Oaks, CA: SAGE.

This text by two of the pioneers of grounded theory has wide application for understanding qualitative research based on interview and focus group data, such as is the focus of this book.

Ritchie, J and Lewis, J (2006) *Qualitative Research Practice: A guide for social science students and researchers*. London: SAGE.

This textbook is particularly good on the philosophy of 'knowing' and on the generalisability of qualitative research.

Spencer, L, Ritchie, J, Lewis, J and Dillon, L (2003) *Quality in Qualitative Evaluation: A framework for assessing research evidence*. London: Cabinet Office.

This is a valuable book for understanding the challenges in developing a framework for evaluating qualitative studies. The team does not give up on the challenge and adopts a 'middle-of-the-road' approach, having described the poles of views on appraising qualitative research and the tensions between them.

Chapter 7

Appraising studies of effectiveness

Introduction

A primary focus for research for the social work profession is testing the effectiveness of interventions designed to achieve beneficial change for clients, families, groups and communities. Ethically, it is wrong to waste the time and energies of service recipients in interventions with little or no effect. Professional decisions about interventions need to be justified and based on sound evidence (Taylor, 2013). Hence, a primary focus of research in social work has to be on determining the effectiveness of interventions. As the International Federation of Social Workers notes, *Social work bases its methodology on a systematic body of evidence-based knowledge derived from research and practice evaluation* (IFSW, 2000, p1). This chapter addresses the challenges and opportunities facing social work in appraising the quality of studies of effectiveness of social work interventions.

The profession needs to be able to demonstrate the effectiveness of its psychosocial interventions if it is to receive funding support through governments and charitable bodies (Bloom et al., 2009; Fischer, 1973). This is leading to a small but increasing urgency to the need to appraise not just effectiveness but cost-effectiveness (Knapp, 2007). Cost-effectiveness requires the development of a new dimension of knowledge and skill in social care (Layard et al., 2007) and is beyond the scope of this book.

The focus of this chapter is on how to measure the effectiveness of a social work intervention. People's perceptions of intervention processes have uses (see Chapter 6) but are insufficient to measure effectiveness, and may on occasion be misleading. Consider, for example, the attitudes of some parents after a compulsory intervention to protect their children from abuse or the perspective of some mental health clients during and after a compulsory admission to psychiatric hospital for assessment during a crisis. Strong feelings as gathered by qualitative research do not give a useful measure of effectiveness in themselves, although they may contribute a useful insight into the helping process.

As outlined in Chapter 3, experimental and quasi-experimental designs are strong research designs suited to studying the effectiveness of a planned intervention. This chapter begins by general considerations of the quality of studies designed to measure the effectiveness of social care interventions, followed by a brief outline of the main study types that are of most interest for this type of research question. The chapter goes on to consider in turn the ten quality appraisal questions as outlined in the QAT-E: Quality Appraisal Tool: (Quasi-)Experimental studies in Appendix 3. General discussion of the appraisal of research quality relevant to studies of effectiveness is in Chapter 5. The chapter concludes by considering some of the challenges for social work in relation to robust randomised trial studies of effectiveness.

Priorities in the design of a study of effectiveness

The main focus in research on the effectiveness of social work interventions is on whether the outcome observed among clients after undertaking the intervention was caused by that intervention. The main focus is therefore on **internal validity** – that is, on whether other possible causes of the observed change can been eliminated as causes. We would want to know whether the outcome was measured in an unbiased and valid way, but also we will be particularly interested in the overall study design so as to be able to eliminate confounding factors that might have contributed to the change. We want to know whether the apparent effect is attributable to chance or whether we can reliably claim that the intervention itself caused the change. There are also considerations of **external validity** – that is, whether the results are applicable in other contexts. In particular, if the study has been conducted in some way that is unrealistic compared to everyday life, then questions about external validity will address concerns about transferability of the intervention to more realistic contexts. In order to develop our understanding, we will start by considering simple designs and work towards more robust designs by adding greater complexity to address identified issues.

Outline of experimental and quasi-experimental methods

The simplest way that we might approach evaluating an intervention would be to administer some type of measuring scale at the end of the intervention. This would seek to measure some key aspects of the behaviours of the client or family that the intervention was designed to address. The most obvious weakness of this approach is that we do not know the level the participants would have scored at the beginning of the intervention, so it is not possible to say very much about the effect of the intervention itself.

In a before-and-after – also called pre-and-post-test – design, the outcome measure is used with the clients or families both before and after the intervention in order to measure change. This is stronger than only gathering data after the intervention. However, a study using this design cannot conclude with certainty that any change observed is attributable to the intervention. There may be other changes occurring to these families (for example, social events in the neighbourhood, changes in government policy or general economic decline or improvement) causing the observed change or, indeed, negating the effectiveness of the intervention.

Research Example

A before-and-after design

This service evaluation examined measuring outcomes in day care and in particular endeavoured to identify if there is a significant change in participants' perceived levels of stress and mental health, after participating in a Positive Living Programme designed to help improve mental well-being. The Perceived Stress Scale (PSS) to measure perceived levels of stress and the Schwartz Outcome Scale (SOS10) to measure the effectiveness of mental health treatment were used in a before-and-after study to measure change from admission to the day centre to the end of the programme 16 weeks later.

Fifty-one day centre members across six day centres completed the tools at the start; 37 of these completed the tools at the end. A paired-sample t-test was conducted to evaluate the impact of the intervention on service-user scores. There was a statistically significant decrease in PSS scores (improvement) from Time 1 (Mean = 24.59, SD = 6.38) to Time 2 (Mean = 18.89, SD = 5.35), $t(36) = 5.35$, $p < .001$, (two-tailed). The mean decrease in the PSS scores was 5.70 with a 95% confidence interval ranging from 3.54 to 7.87. The eta squared statistic (0.44) indicated a large effect size. There was a statistically significant increase (improvement) in SOS10 from time 1 (M = 27.86, SD = 13.45) to Time 2 (M = 38.19, SD = 11.89), $t(36) = 3.87$, $p < .001$ (two-tailed). The mean increase in SOS10 scores was 10.32 with a 95% confidence interval ranging from 15.73 to −3.87. The eta squared statistic (0.29) indicated a large effect size. These two measures were effective and useful in demonstrating client outcomes in the Positive Living Programme. This project demonstrated the viability of using validated scales to measure client outcomes in a low-intensity day care programme, encouraging the use of validated scales to measure outcomes for other day care programmes and in other social care settings.

(Gillespie, 2014)

Quasi-experimental designs

In order to address this fundamental issue of the cause of the observed change, a variety of experimental and quasi-experimental research designs have been developed. Quasi-experimental studies are where the researcher has some control over which people receive the intervention or else over how a control group is created, but where participants are not allocated randomly.

A non-randomised controlled intervention design may be appropriate where it is possible to measure the participants both before and after the intervention, but not influence which received the intervention. For example, a control group might be identified comprising individuals (or families) in a broadly similar situation to those in the intervention group. This provides some additional rigour by comparison with the simple pre-post studies outlined above. However, a weakness is the factors on which the pairs are created may not represent all the relevant factors. Also, inevitably, there will be limitations of what can reasonably be achieved in terms of degree of matching in relation to the number of clients or families available from which to select. The appraisal of quality of non-randomised controlled studies is discussed more fully in Deeks et al. (2003).

An interrupted time series (ITS) design is where multiple observations are made over a period of time, where there are periods with and without intervention. The design focuses on the likelihood that the response to an intervention will probably be stronger while the intervention is being carried out (or increase during the intervention) and is likely then to reduce when the intervention stops. Measurements at appropriate points could identify these changing levels of response, and thus give a measure of the effectiveness of the intervention. It is traditional to describe the measures before the intervention as time A and the measures during the intervention as time B. As an example, one might measure the level of a family problem before the parenting programme (time A), then measure it again during the intervention (time B). After the programme finishes (time A again), the level of the problem could be measured again. A gradual reduction in the effect of the programme over time would be expected. The intervention could be repeated (time B again) at a later date, giving an A–B–A–B design which, as a design, would be more convincing than the simpler A–B or A–B–A design where the effect observed was due to the intervention rather than other factors. The ITS design is particularly suited to identifying the aspects of interventions influencing outcomes. The ITS is a design suited to identifying variables and developing the understanding of principles of effective practice, whereas the experimental designs below are better suited to testing the overall effectiveness of interventions. ITS designs are also suited to community interventions.

Experimental designs

It will be apparent that the above designs suffer from weaknesses in not fully addressing the need to ensure that all factors are taken into account in order to ensure that the outcomes being measured are caused by the intervention. Thus, we progress in complexity of research design to studies where participants are allocated randomly between whether they receive the intervention or not. This is called a randomised controlled intervention study, or randomised controlled trial. If people are allocated randomly, then they each have an equal chance of being allocated to the group receiving the intervention or to the control group. Hence, with enough participants the group receiving the intervention and the control group will, on average, be similar in every relevant respect. Thus, any effect can be attributed with confidence to the intervention and not to any other factor.

There are various types of experimental designs. The simplest form of a randomised controlled intervention study is to have two parallel 'groups', one of which receives the intervention and one of which does not. Note that in this context the word 'group' does not imply people meeting together, but simply that all these people in a 'group' receive the same intervention (or no intervention). A slightly more complex design is to have two groups each receiving a different intervention. Sometimes a design might have three groups, such as two receiving different interventions and one receiving no intervention.

Research Example

Randomised controlled intervention study

This article discusses the effectiveness of a multicomponent intervention designed to disrupt developmental processes associated with conduct problems and peer rejection in childhood. Compared with 41 children randomised to a wait list control condition, 45 children in an intervention condition received a social skills training programme. At the same time, their parents participated in an in-home family intervention. Compared with control group children, intervention children demonstrated significant improvements on five of six outcome measures. Differences between the experimental and control groups suggest the programmes strengthen children's prosocial behaviour, promote their ability to regulate emotions, and increase social contact with peers. Intervention was associated also with significant improvements in classroom comportment and decreases in relational aggression, a measure of coercion in peer relationships. The findings are consistent with those of other programmes effective in interrupting risk processes associated with conduct problems in childhood and early adolescence.

(Fraser et al., 2004)

There are variants on this randomised controlled intervention design. A cluster randomised controlled design is where clusters rather than individuals are randomised. Thus, for example, a list of social work locality offices might be compiled and the offices randomly allocated as to whether they are experimental or control. The social workers in the experimental locality offices are then trained in the intervention while those in the control localities are not. The results are measured in terms of individual clients or families, although the randomisation was not at the level of individuals or families but at the level of 'clusters' of clients according to social work locality offices.

Research Example

Cluster randomised intervention study

Background: *Falls and resulting injuries are particularly common in older people living in residential care facilities, but knowledge about the prevention of falls is limited.*

Objective: *To investigate whether a multi-dimensional intervention program would reduce falls and fall-related injuries.*

Design: *A cluster randomised, controlled, non-blinded trial.*

Setting: *9 residential care facilities located in a northern Swedish city.*

Clients: *439 residents 65 years of age or older.*

Intervention: *An 11-week multi-professional program included general and resident-specific, tailored strategies. The strategies comprised educating staff, modifying the environment, implementing exercise programs, supplying and repairing aids, reviewing drug regimes, providing free hip protectors, having post-fall problem-solving conferences and guiding staff.*

Measurements: *The primary outcomes were the number of residents sustaining a fall, the number of falls and the time to occurrence of the first fall. A secondary outcome was the number of injuries resulting from falls.*

Results: *During the 34-week follow-up period, 82 residents (44%) in the intervention program sustained a fall compared with 109 residents (56%) in the control group (risk ratio, 0.78 [95% CI, 0.64 to 0.96]). The adjusted odds ratio was 0.49 (CI, 0.37 to 0.65), and the adjusted incidence rate ratio of falls was 0.60 (CI, 0.50 to 0.73). Each of three residents in the intervention group and 12 in the control group had a femoral fracture (adjusted odds ratio, 0.23 [CI, 0.06 to 0.94]). Clustering was considered in all regression models.*

Conclusion: *A multi-professional and multi-dimensional prevention program targeting residents, staff, and the environment may reduce falls and femoral fractures.*

(Jensen et al., 2002, p733)

The cluster randomised controlled design can be useful to avoid the possibility of 'contamination' between participants providing the intervention and those who are the control. In some circumstances, this may be the only feasible experimental approach for this reason. For example, if the intervention were randomised on an individual level, those social workers being trained to deliver the new intervention might talk informally with those providing a service to those individuals in the control group. Thus, those providing a service to the control group might unwittingly adopt some of the ideas or practices of the planned new intervention the researchers are trying to measure as being the essential difference between the two groups. Clarity about the essential difference in the intervention between the groups makes it possible to understand how effective the intervention is for future practice. A cluster randomised controlled design requires a larger sample than the standard randomised trial design because there are factors between clusters to be balanced as well as those at participant level and a good quality study should take account of this (Everitt et al., 2001).

There are ethical issues to consider in using randomisation, as the group receiving the intervention may be regarded as being favoured compared to the control group. Equally the intervention group might be regarded as being put at greater risk from an intervention of unknown effectiveness. Using a waiting-list control method is often an ethically acceptable approach to randomisation in studies of the effectiveness of social work interventions. In essence, both groups will receive the intervention, but one group will not.

Research Summary

Use of waiting list control group

Objective: *To evaluate the effectiveness of cognitive therapy for post-traumatic stress disorder related to terrorism and other civil conflict in Northern Ireland.*

Design: *Randomised controlled trial managed by a social worker.*

Setting: *Team led by a social worker at a community treatment centre.*

Participants: *58 consecutive clients with chronic post-traumatic stress disorder (median 5.2 years, range 3 months to 32 years) mostly resulting from multiple traumas linked to terrorism and other civil conflict (primarily the Omagh bombing).*

Interventions: *To determine whether cognitive therapy was more effective than no treatment, at 12 weeks clients allocated to immediate cognitive therapy were compared with clients allocated to the waiting list condition. This was done because the researchers anticipated that many of the clients referred to the centre would be those who had failed more commonly available psychological treatments, such as counselling or debriefing, or pharmacotherapy. A design comparing cognitive therapy with alternative treatments would have excluded such people. Also, cognitive therapy has already been shown to be superior to supportive counselling in non-terrorism-related post-traumatic stress disorder. Potential clients would have been on a waiting list to receive cognitive therapy for longer than 12 weeks at this time, due to demand on this publicly-funded service. Those on the waiting list received treatment subsequent to the period of study. Treatment comprised a mean of 5.9 sessions during 12 weeks and 2.0 sessions thereafter.*

Outcome Measures: *Primary outcome measures were clients' scores for post-traumatic stress disorder (post-traumatic stress diagnostic scale) and depression (Beck Depression Inventory). The secondary outcome measures were scores for occupational and social functioning (work related disability, social disability, and family-related disability) on the Sheehan Disability Scale.*

Results: *At 12 weeks after randomisation, immediate cognitive therapy was associated with significantly greater improvement than the waiting list control group in the symptoms of post-traumatic stress disorder (mean difference 9.6, 95% confidence interval 3.6 to 15.6), depression (mean difference 10.1, 4.8 to 15.3), and self-reported occupational and social functioning (mean difference 1.3, 0.3 to 2.5). Effect sizes from before to after treatment were large: post-traumatic stress disorder 1.25, depression 1.05, and occupational and social functioning 1.17. No change was observed in the control group.*

Conclusion: *Cognitive therapy is an effective treatment for post-traumatic stress disorder related to terrorism and other civil conflict.*

(Duffy et al., 2007, p1147)

Hierarchy of evidence

There is widespread recognition of a *hierarchy of evidence* (McNeese and Thyer, 2004; NICE, 2005) which rank orders the quality of research design (such as those outlined above) of studies to measure the effectiveness of planned interventions such as are carried out by social workers. This hierarchy is widely accepted among researchers internationally (Petticrew and Roberts, 2006). The hierarchy of evidence does not purport to address quality issues in relation to other research questions for which other research designs may be more appropriate (see Chapter 3). This

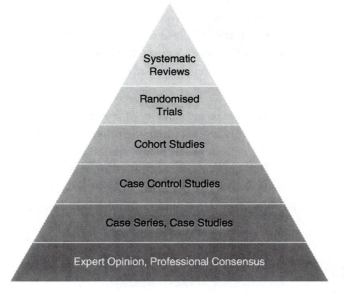

Figure 7.1   Hierarchy of design for quality of studies of effectiveness of an intervention

(see Centre for Reviews and Dissemination (2009) and other versions) hierarchy of evidence does not address other issues of quality of experimental studies such as the quality of the data collection tools or the way they are administered. There is some debate about this hierarchy, although the criticisms are almost entirely by people who misunderstand its tightly defined purpose and scope. It might be helpful to the debate if a new name could be found to more accurately reflect its purpose! At the present time there are no equivalent widely accepted hierarchies for appraising designs in relation to other types of research question, such as those addressed by surveys and qualitative research (see Chapters 5 and 6), although there have been various attempts (e.g. Downs and Black, 1998; Farrington, 2003; Taylor et al., 2007a).

Rationale for the study

Having considered general features of the design of studies of effectiveness, we now turn our attention to specific questions that might be asked to appraise quality. As with other research questions and designs, a study of effectiveness needs to have a clearly formulated question, aims and objectives. The question should be developed from a review of existing research and theory so as to demonstrate the robustness of the concepts used. This ensures that the study can most effectively build on existing knowledge.

Study design

The study design should have an explicit and valid rationale, using the principles outlined above in terms of differences between designs. There should be an acceptable statement about measures taken to ensure consistency in the delivery of the intervention. This is generally known as **intervention fidelity**, and means that the intervention must be defined sufficiently clearly and that variations in how it is delivered are within acceptable limits.

There are various threats to the internal validity of studies of effectiveness such as contemporaneous events (e.g. some incident with high emotional impact on participants) and the passage of time (such as maturation of participants over the duration of the study). A full randomised controlled intervention study will by its design have addressed these issues. For the other variants described above, these threats to validity need to be considered, and might usefully be referred to in the study report.

Sampling

The method of sampling should be clearly described. This should include the main characteristics of the participants as well as brief information about the setting for delivering the intervention. A **random sample** is by definition an essential component of an experimental study. Even where there is random allocation, it is good practice to provide data on the intervention and control groups in terms of how similar they are at the start of the study. The essential principle is to reduce **selection bias**, that is, to reduce the likelihood that those people receiving the intervention of interest are different in any relevant characteristic from those in whom we compare the outcome.

A key aspect of a study of effectiveness is to ascertain whether any difference between the group that received the intervention and the participants in the control group is simply caused by chance variation between the participants involved. How likely is it that the difference is simply 'chance'? We use the concept of **statistical significance** for this. By convention, it is common to define a study as statistically significant if there is only a 1 in 20 (5 per cent) likelihood that the result (i.e. the difference between the groups) could have been obtained by chance. Three factors affect the statistical significance of results:

1. the variation in the characteristic being measured among the population studied;

2. the precision of the measures of this characteristic; and

3. the sample size.

A good quality study will have a statement about the calculation of the sample size necessary to achieve statistical significance.

There may be people invited to participate in a study who refuse to do so. Ideally, a good quality study should have some discussion about recruitment and any refusal to participate, particularly if there are substantial numbers who refuse. Something to check is whether all those entering the study are accounted for at the end. This issue of attrition is discussed further below in relation to analysis of the data.

There is the possibility of the participants or the social workers providing the intervention skewing the results through their actions, either unwittingly or through bias. The researcher must be confident that clients receiving help and those providing help have not confounded the results of the study through attempts to make the intervention being studied appear more or less successful than it really was. In a study involving randomisation, a key quality question is whether allocation was concealed from participants. This is commonly addressed by **blinding** or **masking** the participants to which intervention they were receiving. In medicinal trials this might be done by giving both the intervention and control groups identical-looking tablets, although only those tablets given to the intervention group would contain the active ingredient under study. This is often more problematic in social work interventions than in healthcare interventions. Participants in a psycho-social helping process have to engage consciously in that process. If families have any experience of services they will know the difference between a novel family group conferencing approach and the way the social worker has previously handled this type of situation. Therapeutic psycho-social interventions, such as varieties of counselling and group work, are influenced by client motivation and as an ethical principle social workers normally explain the proposed intervention to prospective clients.

Ethical aspects

To know about the effectiveness of social work interventions, the rationale for using some type of experimental or quasi-experimental design, as outlined above, is overwhelming, other aspects of quality being equal. With rigorous intervention research, it is possible to gain sound evidence of the effectiveness of interventions so social workers are not wasting time and resources of clients, organisations, the profession and society with activities unlikely to be productive. There are a number of ethical issues to be addressed in relation to using experimental studies in social work. Research ethics committees now consider poor science to be poor ethics. In other words, a design inefficient for its purposes is unethical since it would impose an inappropriate burden on participants in relation to the expected value to be derived from it, in addition to the ethical issues in the proper use of resources by the funding body (Taylor, 2012a).

Any study of the effectiveness of an intervention should have a statement about the mechanism for receiving research ethics approval from an appropriate body. Because of the pressure on word length in typical journal articles, readers may be disappointed at the limited information available about ethical issues. Much of this is assumed within the rigorous processes now required in many countries for research ethics approval. It is generally assumed that within these procedures issues of informed consent and confidentiality are approved to a high standard. Journals will often require a statement about any conflict of interest.

There is a broader ethical issue for studies of effectiveness in terms of 'depriving' one group (the control group) of an intervention which might be of value to them. The other side of the discussion has to be about the dangers or waste of time that might be involved if the intervention is not effective. It is only through robust studies that we will ascertain whether or not an intervention is of any use. The general view at present is that an experimental or quasi-experimental study would be justifiable morally if we have sufficient knowledge to believe that the new intervention might work and is safe enough, but that we do not know enough to justify saying that we know it is effective. There is also an argument that the study would be justified in terms of the welfare of future clients, who would thereby be offered a more knowledgeable and effective service. This professional consensus approach to this aspect of ethics needs to be developed more fully in social work.

A common approach to this ethical issue of depriving people of an intervention is to use waiting list controls (see pages 102–3). If people were on a waiting list for a service, then they might be picked at random to receive the service more quickly, while those not picked would be regarded as the control group who would receive the same service in due time. In this case none would be disadvantaged by the study taking place by comparison with the service that they would have received, although some might be advantaged. Another approach to this ethical issue is that the control group receives the normal intervention, as opposed to the traditional no intervention. This standard is now being introduced in medical trials and is viewed generally as more acceptable in terms of social work ethics. It should be noted, however, with this approach that the new intervention needs to be sufficiently more effective than normal practice to demonstrate a significant effect. This presents even more challenge to social work in terms of outcome measures fine enough to differentiate between the levels of outcome.

There are ethical and legal issues for social work intervention studies if the new process being tested involves by-passing standard procedures. For example, if we wish to test a new family-oriented intervention for child protection, it might involve families in the intervention group not going through the standard child-protection procedures.

The ideal for good social work research is to engage key stakeholders at each stage of the process, to ensure that there will be value not just for the researcher but also for managers and practitioners as well as clients and families. This is discussed further in the INVOLVE literature (see Further Reading, Chapter 1). One ethical issue is respecting the choices of participants. Generally speaking, clients allocated to the intervention group can, of course, refuse to participate, and would revert to receiving either no service or the normal service. This is discussed further in the section below on analysis.

Data collection

A critical issue for intervention studies is the use of meaningful and effective tools to measure the change which may be attributable to the intervention. The methods for data collection should be described in sufficient detail for the reader to appraise their quality, if necessary by following up citations to studies about the development of the measurement tools. A good quality study will discuss the relevance, validity and reliability of data collection tool(s) used. Social work goals, such as better family functioning where there has been abuse or discord, or a more independent, satisfying life for a person with disability or in older age, are not as readily measured as, for example, recovery from medical conditions or educational achievements.

Research Summary

Use of outcome measures

Diggle et al. (2002) reviewed studies of parent-mediated early intervention for young children with autism spectrum disorder. The outcomes they measured included child's language progress; child's positive behavioural change; parent interaction style; parent confidence; and reduction in levels of parental stress.

In social work the outcomes of real interest may on occasions be of low incidence or hard to measure. In such circumstances proxy outcome measures may be used. These are measures that are easier to measure robustly, and which give an indication of effectiveness in relation to the outcome that is the main concern.

Research Summary

Proxy outcome measures

In a community-based scheme to help young adults with disabilities to gain employment, the measures used to evaluate effectiveness included:

- *number gaining paid employment (true outcome measure);*
- *number gaining voluntary employment or entering an education or training scheme;*
- *number of qualifications gained (proxy outcome measures);*
- *number of work-experience placements undertaken in relation to the number of participants on the scheme (scheme output measures).*

The number gaining paid employment was low, and it gave a more useful profile of the effectiveness of community-based interventions (such as personal assistants for young adults with physical disability, coaching for young adults with mental health problems, relevant short courses, and supervised work placements) to use a range of proxy outcome measures in addition to the primary measure of interest.

(Taylor et al., 2004)

One approach to outcome measurement in intervention research is to use standardised psychometric scales measuring a particular attribute or behaviour, such as knowledge, ability, personality, motivation, attitudes and social functioning. Examples of well-known standardised scales widely used in social work research and practice include the Beck Depression Inventory (BDI), the General Health Questionnaire (GHQ) and the Mini-Mental State Examination (MMSE).

There has been steady development of quality of life measures to evaluate the general social well-being of individuals and communities. Quality of life measures include objective dimensions, such as physical and mental health, symptoms of the 'problem' or 'issue' bringing the person to the attention of a social worker, and ability to function in terms of daily living, including employment, education and housing. Quality of life measures may include more subjective dimensions focusing on the individual's sense of well-being or life satisfaction. This may include their sense of satisfaction with the domains of work and social engagement as well as overall measures of social well-being. Quality of life tools increasingly embody clients' subjective perceptions of their well-being.

Research Summary

Using a psychometric outcome measure

Sixty-seven mental health staff (including social workers, nurses, occupational therapists and day-care workers) completed a 38-item questionnaire that contained four scales measuring organisational change, self-efficacy, role conflict and role ambiguity. Results showed that there were strong negative correlations between organisational climate and role stressors, and a negative correlation of moderate significance between self-efficacy and role ambiguity. Implications for organisations and practice were drawn out (MacAteer et al., 2015).

Another dimension of the quality of an experimental or quasi-experimental study is the objectivity of those measuring participants at the start and end of the study. Additional rigour can be achieved if those doing the measurements do not know to which group participants belonged (detection bias). This can address the possibility of bias among members of the research team. Researchers who are also practitioners might stand to gain financially or in terms of prestige if 'their treatment' is shown to be effective. Conversely, those with a vested interest in a particular intervention might stand to lose their living or prestige if 'their intervention' is not shown to be effective. Such motivations may bias the measurements taken. Such bias may not be apparent in the measuring tool itself, but might only be apparent in the context in which it was administered. For example, the instructions given to participants regarding how to complete the form may bias their responses. Although the masking of participants in a study is often problematic for psycho-social interventions, the masking of the researchers measuring participants is readily achieved.

Data analysis

The method of analysis of the data should be outlined in the methods section of the paper. It should be clearly described, although a level of statistical knowledge may be assumed as the word-count is restrictive and many readers might regard such material as stating the obvious. You should consult with a textbook on research methods if you are unsure of the statistical aspects of the methodology. The method of analysis should be justified, although again this may present challenges to those less comfortable with statistics. In general, you might assume quality in this dimension in that publications in peer-reviewed journals have been through a rigorous peer-review process including statistical review.

A key quality issue is whether the planned intervention is the only difference between the experiences of the intervention and control groups. This is known as **performance bias** and can be an important factor in psycho-social interventions as incidental aspects of the environment for the intervention may have an effect.

Research Summary

Allowance for confounding factors

Context: *As the population ages the number of people in our communities suffering with dementia is rising. This affects the quality of life of people with dementia and also increases the burden on family caregivers, community care and residential care services. Exercise is one lifestyle factor that has been identified as a potential means of reducing or delaying progression of the symptoms of dementia.*

Study characteristics: *This review evaluated the results of 17 trials including 1,067 participants that tested whether exercise programmes could improve cognition (including things such as memory, reasoning ability and spatial awareness), activities of daily living, behaviour and psychological symptoms (such as depression, anxiety and agitation) in older people with dementia. We also looked for effects on mortality, quality of life, caregivers' experience and use of healthcare services, and for any adverse effects of exercise.*

Types of interventions: *Interventions included exercise programmes offered over any length of time with the aim of improving cognition, activities of daily living, neuropsychiatric symptoms, depression, and mortality in older people with dementia or improving the family caregiver's burden, health, quality of life, or to decrease caregiver mortality, or use of health and care services, or a combination of these. We included trials where the only difference between groups was the exercise intervention, and the types, frequencies, intensities, duration and settings of the exercise programmes were described. The exercise could be any combination of aerobic-, strength-, or balance-training. The comparison groups received either usual care, or social contact and activities, to ensure that the participants received a similar amount of attention.*

Findings: *There was evidence that exercise programmes can improve the ability of people with dementia to perform daily activities, but there was much unexplained variation among results. The studies showed no evidence of benefit from exercise on cognition, psychological symptoms or depression. There was little evidence regarding the other outcomes listed. There was no evidence that exercise was harmful for the participants. The overall quality of evidence behind most of the results was very low.*

Conclusion: *Additional well-designed trials would allow us to enhance the quality of the review by investigating the best type of exercise programmes for people with different types and severity of dementia and by addressing all of the outcomes.*

(Forbes et al., 2015)

One source of error is if participants drop out of receiving the intervention – known as **attrition bias**. For example, some participants in the intervention group drop out of receiving a service. If the control group is defined as those receiving no service, then these people might be regarded as belonging to the control group. In analysing data, the most rigorous studies handle this in terms of *intention to treat*, where data on participants is included in the group to which they were originally allocated. This provides a more rigorous test of the effectiveness of the intervention than if their data was removed from the study.

A central issue is the size of the effect that is attributable to the intervention. It is all very well to have an effect that is found to be statistically significant (see page 105), but if the size of the effect is small, the value of the intervention for practice will be limited. A good quality study will report not only statistical significance in terms of probability that the outcome was not attributable to chance. It will also report on the **effect size** so that the importance of the results for practice may be judged. The effect size will be expressed in terms of change in the characteristic being measured.

Presentation of findings

There should be a clear statement of the results, and these should clearly address the research question posed. Increasingly, there is an expectation that studies of effectiveness will also include some consideration of costs and cost-effectiveness, although this is little developed at present in relation to psycho-social interventions. If there are any null or negative outcomes it is still valuable that these are published, but there should be some discussion reporting the views of the researchers on this.

Credibility of findings

Do not forget common sense when appraising research. Ask yourself whether the findings seem credible. Imagine the research process from the perspective of participants and ask yourself about their experience of what was happening. The discussion section of a journal article normally commences with a paragraph about the limitations of the study. This should be an honest statement of the key weaknesses in the study. There are many pitfalls to carrying out randomised controlled trials and quasi-experimental studies in social work (Coulter, 2011).

In terms of the theoretical framework and discussion, are the explanations (models) presented plausible and coherent? Social work interventions are often complex and take place in complex environments (Medical Research Council, 2008). Factors such as multiple stressors, multiple problems (co-morbidities), poverty and strained relationships with family and neighbours create a complexity presenting challenges to the design, development and evaluation of effective interventions. Such complexity might be described in terms of the multidimensional, interacting components, the complex behaviours required of providers and recipients of the intervention, the levels targeted (individual, group and organisational), the variability and unpredictability of outcomes, and the flexibility often demanded in practice to tailor interventions to particular circumstances. Without being unduly unsympathetic to the range of theoretical approaches that are possible, there needs to be some appraisal of the coherence and plausibility of the understanding presented of the meaning of the study findings.

Discussion and conclusions

The study should draw some conclusions that are robustly based on the data presented. More speculative comments should be clearly identified as such. The findings should be discussed in the light of the literature presented as contextual material earlier in the paper. There should be some account of how these findings confirm or contradict previous research. Alternative explanations for the findings should be explored and discounted in some way. The contribution of this particular study to the broader development of knowledge in this field should be articulated in some way.

Generalisability to other settings

The final questions to ask are the extent to which the findings of the study are transferable to other settings. Were the subjects similar in important respects to those of interest to you? Was the context similar to or different from your own setting? How applicable are the findings to practice or policy in another country with its configuration of culture, legislation, services, policies and politics?

Generalisability of experimental studies is not based on the statistical representativeness of the sample from which participants are drawn, as it would be for a survey. Nor does it relate to the development of a theoretical construct as in qualitative research. The main quality issue addressed in (quasi-)experimental studies is internal validity: the extent to which confounding factors are eliminated as explanations for the observed change. The generalisability of a (quasi-)experimental study may be little discussed in the article. The reader will need to make some appraisal of the similarity of the participants and the viability in another setting of the intervention used.

Challenges in studying effectiveness

The use of evidence to inform practice has been the essence of social work since its beginnings. This is particularly important in terms of evidence about the effectiveness of interventions. Professional social workers need to make judgements about how to intervene with individuals and families, and these judgements need to be based on the best knowledge available. When people talk of an intervention, in any area of life, as being 'effective', they do not mean, of course, that the intervention will be 'successful' in every situation. For example, a medication being regarded as effective for headaches does not mean that every headache for every person will cease the moment they take this medication. What should now be clearer from reading this chapter is that 'effective' means that there is a statistically significant improvement in the condition of interest between an experimental group that undertakes the treatment of interest and a control group that does not.

The approach to quality appraisal in this book follows a multidimension, holistic approach as outlined in the Introduction. There are challenges in drawing a threshold line in terms of good-enough quality for inclusion in a review. This applies to any research question and study design, not just studies of effectiveness as discussed in this chapter. The most straightforward approach for appraising studies of effectiveness is in terms of design using the hierarchy of evidence. A parallel approach in terms of studies using diverse designs is discussed in Chapter 8. Reliance on design as the only determinant of a threshold of quality for inclusion of the study in a review is premised on two factors. First, the research design is fundamental; issues of sampling and measurement are to no avail if the fundamental design is weak. Second, with the major expenditure and rigorous ethical approval required for experimental studies on humans, it can reasonably be assumed that sound approaches have been used to sample size and outcome measures in these studies. In general, the 'building blocks' will have been carefully constructed to create an effective experimental study, although in social work this can present many challenges (Coulter, 2011).

Becoming a social worker

Being able to appraise research that has used an experimental or quasi-experimental method is a valuable skill for the professional social worker, not least because this is a weakness generally in social work research in Europe. It is important that professionals in the field are able to discern the quality of such papers and the extent to which they gather valid data to inform practice. This chapter relates particularly to domain 5.11 of the PCF on demonstrating an understanding of experimental and quasi-experimental research methods.

Reflection Point

How does this type of knowledge of effectiveness inform your practice?

Activity 7.1

Evidence into practice task

- Search a database to identify a paper reporting a study that asked a question about the effectiveness of a social work intervention and which used experimental methods.
- Use the appraisal tool QAT-E: Quality Appraisal Tool: (Quasi-)Experimental studies in Appendix 3 to extract key information about the methods used and to learn to appraise the quality of an experimental or quasi-experimental study.

> ## Chapter Summary
>
> - The main features of the major types of experimental and quasi-experimental study have been outlined and the rationale for their design explained in terms of eliminating confounding factors that might otherwise account for the effects observed.
> - The hierarchy of evidence for the design of experimental and quasi-experimental studies addressing questions of effectiveness of interventions is explained.
> - The ten main questions in the QAT-E: Quality Appraisal Tool: (Quasi-)Experimental studies in Appendix 4 have been discussed in turn in order to guide appraisal of studies of effectiveness.
> - Some of the challenges for social work in achieving high quality studies of effectiveness are discussed in relation to the main design points of randomised controlled studies.

Further Reading

Centre for Reviews and Dissemination (CRD) (2009) *Systematic Reviews: CRD's guidance for undertaking reviews in health care* (3rd edition). University of York: CRD. Available at: www.york.ac.uk/crd/

CRD is a research department that specialises in evidence synthesis, assembling and analysing data from multiple research studies to generate policy-relevant research. It undertakes high quality systematic reviews and associated economic evaluations, develops underpinning methods, and promotes and facilitates the use of research evidence in decision making. Over the past 20 years the department has completed over 160 systematic reviews covering a wide range of health and care topics, many of which have had a direct impact on national policy. CRD provides methodological guidance on systematic reviewing of the effectiveness of health and care interventions.

Downs, S and Black, N (1998) The feasibility of creating a checklist for the assessment of the methodological quality of both randomised and non-randomised studies of healthcare interventions. *Journal of Epidemiology and Community Health,* 52: 377–84.

This is a valuable paper on appraising studies of the effectiveness of care and treatment interventions in the community.

Fischer, J and Corcoran, K (2007) *Measures for Clinical Practice and Research: A sourcebook. Vol. 1: Couples, families, and children.* New York: Oxford University Press.

Fischer, J and Corcoran, K (2007) *Measures for Clinical Practice and Research: A sourcebook. Vol. 2: Adults.* New York: Oxford University Press.

These two volumes provide an excellent compendium of assessment tools specifically for social workers to use in their practice with individuals, couples and families. The term 'clinical social work' is common in North America and Australasia to denote social workers helping individuals and groups to tackle psycho-social problems, rather than community development, safeguarding or care planning aspects of social work.

Rubin, A and Bellamy, J (2012) *Practitioner's Guide to Using Research for Evidence-Based Practice* (2nd edition). Hoboken, NJ: Wiley.

This book is recommended for the reader who wishes to explore the topics in this book in more depth, particularly in relation to appraisal of various types of quasi-experimental research design.

Chapter 8

Synthesising research

Introduction

Having identified relevant research on your topic (see Chapters 3 and 4) and decided which relevant studies to include in terms of quality (see Chapters 5, 6 and 7), the next stage of a literature review is to synthesise the findings of included studies. There are broadly three types of approach to synthesising research.

- *Narrative synthesis* – where the results of studies, whether qualitative or quantitative, are combined into a narrative based on their main conclusions.

- *Meta-synthesis* – where the findings of qualitative studies are combined using principles of qualitative research.

- *Meta-analysis* – where the results of quantitative studies are combined quantitatively using explicit statistical principles.

We will use the term synthesis to encompass all three of these approaches to combining studies, and will discuss each of these approaches in turn.

For clarity, we recap that a systematic review is where a review of research has an explicit and robust methodology for all three parts: (1) identification of relevant research, (2) quality appraisal and (3) synthesis (i.e. meta-analysis or meta-synthesis) (Rutter et al., 2010). Where a narrative synthesis is part of a review that has an explicit methodology for identification of relevant research or for quality appraisal, or both, we use the term **systematic narrative review** for the whole (Killick and Taylor, 2009).

This chapter describes these three main approaches to synthesis of literature following an outline of **literature mapping**, which is an approach to getting an overview of the main topics covered by retrieved literature. After the sections on narrative review, meta-synthesis and meta-analysis, we describe the work of participants in the international Cochrane and Campbell Collaborations who undertake systematic reviews of the best evidence of the effectiveness of social care interventions. Finally, we consider ways in which knowledge from a meta-synthesis of qualitative research and a meta-analysis of experimental studies may be brought together to complement each other in building knowledge to inform social work practice.

Selection of studies for synthesis: quality threshold

There are a number of issues in setting a threshold for inclusion of studies in a literature synthesis (Taylor et al., 2007b). It is relatively straightforward to use the hierarchy of evidence (see pages 103–4) in relation to questions of effectiveness of interventions; the question is how far down the hierarchy to go. For a student, this can be adjusted to reflect the number of studies retrieved and the time available. Setting a threshold for inclusion in a review of qualitative studies using a particular method will primarily reflect those that are regarded as coming within the definition of that method. For a narrative synthesis of studies using a range of methods, this question of defining a threshold may also be framed in terms of design. This has parallels with the hierarchy of evidence for appraising studies of effectiveness (experimental and quasi-experimental studies) but using different elements within the schema, as illustrated below.

Research Summary

A hierarchy for narrative synthesis of empirical studies using diverse research designs

Include: *Surveys, qualitative studies, (quasi-)experimental studies.*

Questionable: *Action research, case studies.*

Exclude: *Theoretical, ideological, policy review papers.*

(McFadden et al., 2015)

The dilemma about whether or not to include case studies is that criteria for quality are difficult to define, as outlined in Chapter 3. However, in some instances the distinction between a case study (such as a report by an individual client about his or her experiences) and a small qualitative study (for example, reporting the views of three or four clients about their experiences) may be small. Thus, for some review questions it may be deemed appropriate to include case studies. Similarly, the term **action research** may be used to encompass a wide range of iterative research and quality improvement processes, with varying clarity about the source and credibility of data. In some contexts, part of a study labelled as 'action research' may be regarded as sufficiently robust for inclusion.

It is possible within a larger project to undertake more than one synthesis of data. For example, one might conduct a meta-analysis of a limited number of studies that use very similar methods, together with a narrative review of all studies on the topic. This possibility should be borne in mind in Ph.D. and large-scale literature reviews.

Research Summary

Using more than one type of synthesis

This PhD thesis focused on professional decision making and risk regarding the long term care of older people. A thorough search of four bibliographic databases and hand-searching methods retrieved 22 relevant studies of sufficient quality for inclusion. Two of the included studies used a factorial survey research design involving decision scenarios (vignettes) with randomised factors (Taylor, 2006a) that were presented to respondents. A meta-analysis was carried out in relation to the two factorial survey studies to measure the effect size of specific factors, as well as a narrative synthesis of all 22 studies to give an overview of major themes.

(Taylor, 2004)

Literature mapping

This section explains briefly recent developments in literature mapping and **systematic literature mapping**. These terms are used to describe getting an overview of the general features of the relevant papers retrieved. The distinction between these is the same as the distinction between a review and a systematic review, and between a narrative synthesis and a systematic narrative synthesis. Systematic literature mapping entails having an explicit and justifiable methodology for all three component parts. In practice, the challenges in relation to systematic literature mapping are in relation to study identification, as discussed further below.

Literature mapping exercises can highlight such aspects as developments in the field over time, particular countries that have been active in that aspect of social care research, types of research design used, and strengths and gaps in aspects of the topic that have been studied.

Most often the purpose of searching is to identify a narrow body of literature for synthesis, and this is the major focus of this book. However, sometimes the purpose is to retrieve research on a range of aspects of a topic so as to get a broad overview. The aim may be to identify gaps in the literature or to help in shaping more precise review questions that are relevant to practice and policy. The general approach is to classify studies retrieved by the aspect of the topic that is covered. An example might be searching on a topic such as addiction services and then classifying research retrieved into categories such as access to services, user perspectives on services, effectiveness of services, organisation of services, etc. This 'literature mapping' can be a useful approach to take stock of the existing literature and to identify gaps where there is limited research.

Research Summary

Literature mapping

This literature map provided an overview of research on the extent and impact of mental health problems on families and the acceptability, accessibility and effectiveness of interventions. From an initial retrieval of 13,733 'hits' from searching 20 databases, 10,943 abstracts were screened after the duplicates had been removed and then 754 full documents were categorised by keywords. Included studies addressed the following categories (not mutually exclusive):

- *detection of problems: 220 studies*
- *extent of problems: 197 studies*
- *accessibility of services: 65 studies*
- *acceptability of services: 80 studies*
- *impact of services: 629 studies*
- *effectiveness of services: 150 studies.*

The literature map also identified the country in which each study had taken place, the populations studied in terms of age, sex and some other socio-demographic factors. Where studies focused on specific additional problems this was coded according to 25 categories, such as: alcohol, child neglect, disability, drugs, eating disorder, health promotion and inequalities.

(Bates and Coren, 2006)

A literature mapping exercise based on thorough searching provides a valuable vantage point from which to take stock of the state of research on a topic. One challenge for systematic literature mapping is that to have credibility the search formula must be robust across all the aspects of the topic that are to be included in the mapping exercise. The exercise will have little credibility if the search terms used are inadequate for some dimension of the topic area.

A key task in literature mapping is to formulate a conceptualisation of the dimensions that will be used to classify studies into groups. In social work it would be helpful if the profession could develop an agreed classification relating to aspects of needs and aspects of service provision.

Activity 8.1

Classification schema for literature mapping

Use the following schema to classify papers retrieved on a topic of your choice.

1. Types of presenting psycho-social needs and problems.
2. Prevalence of needs or incidence of the problems.

3. Understanding of the causes (aetiology) of the needs and problems.
4. Service types to address these needs and problems.
5. Availability of services.
6. Accessibility and acceptability of services.
7. Experiences of receiving or participating in services.
8. Experiences of providing or managing services.
9. Processes within services that contribute to effectiveness.
10. Measures of the effectiveness of services for these needs.

Narrative synthesis

The traditional approach to synthesis of creating a coherent narrative that links the studies together is now generally termed a 'narrative synthesis', as a component of a narrative review or systematic narrative review. In essence, the reviewer creates a meaningful narrative from the conclusions of the relevant studies that are of sufficient quality for inclusion. A narrative synthesis may be used regardless of study design, as in essence it takes the main findings and combines these. Where quantitative studies are included in a narrative review, the data are transformed into words that convey the essence of the findings. A narrative review is most often structured according to the major themes or topics within the literature (Popay et al., 2006) and that is our focus here. An alternative is to take a chronological approach, demonstrating the development of ideas over time (Braun and Clarke, 2006).

A common approach to narrative synthesis is first to organise the studies according to categories in terms of topic. The selection of categories may be derived from the retrieved studies only, or may relate to some theoretical framework relevant to the field. Bear in mind that a particular study may contribute to more than one topic. However, be cautious if you find that many studies are cited in more than one topic; it may be that a restructuring of topics would be more effective.

Second, the studies contributing to each category within the topic are synthesised, using the data extracted as described in Chapter 4. Generally, it feels most natural and readable to begin with the study that is the most rigorous and seems to establish a benchmark for other studies within that topic area. This study can then be complemented by descriptions of other studies that confirm a particular aspect of that study or contradict a particular aspect or address a gap. A key challenge is to summarise the essence of each study within the narrative yet also create connections between studies rather than just describing the findings in turn. For reasons of space it is not possible to illustrate the whole of a narrative synthesis here. The reader is referred to narrative reviews published in journals – for example, Agnew et al. (2010); Best et al. (2014a); Hagan et al. (2014); Killick et al. (2015); and McFadden et al. (2015). It will be noted that these recent examples are all systematic narrative reviews – i.e. they include an explicit methodology for study identification. Having an explicit methodology is increasingly becoming a requirement for publication of literature reviews.

Some characteristics of a good narrative synthesis are listed below.

- The focus of the synthesis remains clear throughout.

- The quality of evidence in included papers is evaluated.

- Assumptions in included papers are clarified.

- The commonalities and differences between findings are clarified.

- The potential for new knowledge from combining findings is used.

- A theoretical understanding across studies is created.

- The overall meaning for practice is drawn out across the papers.

Further information on methods of narrative synthesis (primarily related to questions of effectiveness) is available in the guidance document produced by the Economic and Social Research Council (Popay et al., 2006) (see Further Reading section).

Meta-synthesis of qualitative studies

The terminology of narrative synthesis (discussed above) for the traditional relatively unstructured approach to synthesising studies of any study design is now well established, as is the term 'meta-analysis' (discussed below) for the quantitative synthesis of experimental studies. It is becoming increasingly common for the synthesis of qualitative studies using principles derived from qualitative research to be termed 'meta-synthesis' (Walsh and Downe, 2005). This is the terminology used in this book, although it is less well established (see Fisher et al., 2006). The main approaches that are developing for meta-synthesis are outlined in this section.

If there are a number of qualitative studies which gather data using interviews or focus groups, a meta-synthesis can be undertaken to combine the findings of the studies: qualitative meta-synthesis *is an interpretive integration of qualitative findings in primary research reports that are in the form of interpretive syntheses of data: either conceptual-thematic descriptions or interpretive explanations* (Sandelowski and Barroso, 2007, p199). This approach to synthesis adds rigour by comparison with traditional **narrative review**. The focus of meta-synthesis is to represent accurately the constructs of the studies, and to synthesise the findings by thematic groupings (Spencer et al., 2003). One challenge is to try not to lose the appeal of the figures of speech, metaphors and written representations of reality in the original studies. A feature of meta-synthesis compared to a typical narrative review is that greater attention is usually paid to the context and methods of the study, and drawing understandings from this as well as from the findings as presented. A key issue is that the typical journal paper reporting qualitative research often contains too little original data to enable meta-synthesis.

One approach to meta-synthesis is to include only studies that use the same qualitative method. This is perhaps most developed in relation to ethnographic studies, where the term **meta-ethnography** is well established (see, for example, Noblit and Hare, 1988). This is too specialised a topic for this book and the interested reader is referred to Sandelowski and Barroso (2007) in the Further Reading section.

For the purposes of informing social work practice and the development of a knowledge base, it is generally too restrictive to limit ourselves only to qualitative studies using one particular design even though this might provide additional rigour. There are many variants in qualitative methodology, and it is likely that studies using a range of these will be retrieved on a topic suited to qualitative research. Synthesising together only those studies that use just one design would be very restrictive, involve an understanding of the detail of a large number of qualitative methodologies, and require approaches to each of these that are not yet much developed.

What is more useful for an applied discipline such as social work is to develop the synthesis of qualitative studies generally (i.e. across types of qualitative method) but bring in some additional rigour (compared to narrative synthesis) by using general principles of qualitative research. One approach to this type of meta-synthesis of qualitative studies is to use a particular theoretical framework to guide the synthesis (see, for example, Dixon-Woods et al., 2006). This is an underdeveloped field, and the reader interested in exploring these approaches is referred to more detailed texts such as Sandelowski and Barroso (2007) in the Further Reading section.

An exemplar qualitative meta-synthesis published by SCIE (Fisher et al., 2006) illustrates the use of a model of three levels of analysis in a synthesis of qualitative studies.

1. Findings from the primary studies, such as the meanings reported to researchers (sometimes called first-order interpretations).

2. Constructs and interpretations that primary researchers place on these findings (second-order).

3. Explanations and hypotheses developed by reviewers arising from second-order interpretations (third-order).

The use of such a model enables a meta-synthesis not only to summarise the findings of the studies and the insights of the primary researchers, but also to achieve greater insight and development of concepts than in a narrative review.

Research Summary

Levels of analysis in meta-synthesis

Themes from the studies	Primary researcher analysis from the individual study	Reviewer analysis across studies
Will they be 'allowed' home Fear of falling How they will manage or cope Being a burden to others What will have to be given up	Threats: • to future safety and self-sufficiency • to future autonomy • to lifestyle choice Cause anxiety	Higher levels of anxiety associated with higher levels of impairment, and a deteriorating or uncertain trajectory, because of these threats

(Fisher et al., 2006)

Meta-analysis of experimental studies

Having considered general combination of conclusions using narrative synthesis and the meta-synthesis of qualitative studies, we now consider statistical meta-analysis of experimental studies. *The term* meta-analysis, *has come to encompass all of the methods and techniques of quantitative research synthesis* (Lipsey and Wilson, 2001, p1). Studies that are conceptually comparable may be combined in a meta-analysis in order to draw the most robust conclusions across the studies about the size of the effect of the intervention being studied. Most work on meta-analysis has been in relation to experimental and quasi-experimental studies. We comment briefly later on some of the issues in relation to meta-analysis of surveys.

A starting point in combining (quasi-)experimental studies might be to do 'vote counting' – i.e. how many studies show a positive effect of the intervention compared with how many show a negative or no effect. This is a starting point, but clearly it has limitations. One might ask why the studies had contradictory results or very different effect sizes. The size and quality of the samples used by the various studies are ignored in this approach. Those that have smaller or less appropriate samples would be given the same weight as those that have a larger or more appropriate sample (Light and Smith, 1971), which can lead to misleading conclusions.

The origins of meta-analysis lie in the stormy debate raised by Hans Eysenck (1952) when he published a paper arguing that psychological interventions (such as counselling interventions carried out by social workers) have no beneficial effects. In order to assess this claim, Gene V. Glass and Mary Lee Smith statistically standardised and averaged the differences between treatment and control groups (see Chapter 7) across 375 studies of the effectiveness of psycho-therapeutic interventions which was published 25 years later (Smith and Glass, 1977). They called their method 'meta-analysis' and this name has stuck for the statistical aggregation of quantitative research results (Glass et al., 1981). Their conclusion differed from that drawn by Eysenck.

Various approaches have been developed that take into account aspects of the included studies in order to synthesis quantitative data more effectively than by vote counting. Key features of meta-analysis are (1) to create an estimate of the effect size and its confidence interval across all included studies; (2) to calculate whether this treatment (or risk factor) effect is statistically significant compared to 'chance'; and (3) to test whether the variation of the effect across the studies is more than would be expected by chance.

It is important for meta-analysis that the findings of the studies are conceptually comparable – that is, they must deal with sufficiently similar constructs. What is being measured in the studies to be synthesised must be sufficiently similar for synthesis to be meaningful.

Even given similar constructs across studies, there is a challenge in that there will be variations in how these constructs are operationalised and measured. For example, if we were looking at the effectiveness of interventions for depression, we would no doubt identify studies that used various different scales such as Beck's Suicidal Intent Scale or the Hamilton Depression Rating Scale (Fischer and Corcoran, 2007b). Such scales may have different lengths, and a score on one is unlikely to correspond exactly to a similar score on another. Indeed, one scale might be the inverse of another in terms of whether a high score indicates a more severe problem or a healthier individual or relationship. The approach to handling this issue in meta-analysis is normally to use the effect size attributable to the intervention. The direction and magnitude of the effect is measured in terms of **standard deviation** units of the variable under consideration. This relates the mean score on the scale to the range of that variable that occurs in the study. The mean score is divided by the standard deviation of this distribution to give a scale in standard deviation units that is independent of the particular scale being used. Thus, effect size is a statistic that permits us to interpret the values of the variables across studies, and across different measures of those variables (Lipsey and Wilson, 2001, p4).

The aim of this chapter is to introduce the reader to the essential principles that need to be considered in combining statistically the results of studies of effectiveness of interventions and to highlight the rigour of the method. There are challenges to meta-analysis in social work in that although articles usually present sufficient information on participant characteristics, p-values and mean values, even top social work journals sometimes fail to present sufficient information on variance indicators or the precise numbers of participants, which limits the ability to calculate the effect sizes that are essential for meta-analysis (Lundahl et al., 2008). This is one of the challenges facing the profession. For further detail the interested reader is referred to the texts by Lipsey and Wilson (2001), Petticrew and Roberts (2006) or Cooper (1998) for a more detailed description of the art of meta-analysis.

Meta-analysis has been developed to synthesise most effectively and meaningfully the results of experimental and quasi-experimental studies of the effects of a planned intervention. At the present time the methods of meta-analysis have not been developed substantially for synthesis of survey research. One of the reasons for this is the diversity of constructs, measures and samples used in survey research, as well as other challenges in creating a meaningful statistical aggregation for these. Another issue is where statistical significance tests are used, in that these often reflect both the magnitude of the effect and the sampling error. The sampling error around the estimated effect is a function of sample size, and this suffers from what might be regarded as the opposite error to vote counting: giving too much (rather than too little) weight to studies with larger samples.

Cochrane and Campbell Collaboration systematic reviews

Our endeavours to identify relevant studies, appraise their quality and synthesise them are for the purpose of ensuring that we use the best available evidence to inform social work activities. The most rigorous literature reviews are the systematic reviews (Chalmers and Altman, 1995) of the effectiveness of interventions carried out as part of the Cochrane Collaboration (focusing on health and social care interventions) or the Campbell Collaboration (focusing on criminal justice, education, social welfare and international development interventions). These collaborations now involve many thousands of people (see Further Reading section, Chapter 1). The Cochrane Library includes systematic reviews of over 70 interventions that might be carried out by social workers (some requiring post-qualifying training), and there are a number of systematic reviews relevant to our profession in the Campbell Library also.

Research Summary

Some systematic reviews in the Cochrane Library of the effectiveness of interventions that might be carried out or commissioned by a social worker:

- family therapy interventions;
- counselling models, including cognitive behavioural therapy;
- marital therapy for depression;
- psychosocial treatments for deliberate self-harm;
- parenting-training programmes;
- supported housing;
- kinship care;
- supporting foster parents in managing difficult behaviour;
- cognitive stimulation, validation therapy (reality orientation) and narrative review methods (reminiscence) for people with dementia;
- smart home technology for health and social care support.

Activity 8.2

Look up the following systematic review in the Cochrane Online Library:

Martin, S, Kelly, G, Kernohan, WG, McCreight, B and Nugent, C (2008) Smart home technologies for health and social care support. *Cochrane Database of Systematic Reviews*, Issue 4. Art. No.: CD006412; doi: 10.1002/14651858.CD006412.pub2.

- What can you learn about the effectiveness of current smart home technology?
- What further questions remain to be answered?

Combining understandings from qualitative and experimental studies

There have been some exciting developments in qualitative studies being undertaken as part of randomised controlled trials. The value of this can be in optimising the intervention and the way that the study is conducted; helping the trial to be sensitive to the participants; facilitating the interpretation of results; and helping to steer the researchers towards interventions that are more likely to be effective in future trials (O'Cathain et al., 2013). There are also exciting developments in synthesis of qualitative studies being undertaken in parallel with synthesis of experimental studies. One of the most dramatic illustrations of the value of qualitative studies in informing experimental studies is outlined in the following example.

Research Summary

Qualitative meta-synthesis informing a meta-analysis of experimental studies

A research team at the Evidence for Policy and Practice Information and Coordinating Centre (EPPI-Centre) at the University of London undertook a systematic review of the effectiveness of interventions to promote healthy eating among children aged four to ten years. They also undertook a synthesis of qualitative studies on barriers to, and facilitators of, healthy eating amongst the same age group of children. The 33 experimental studies retrieved of effectiveness of interventions were synthesised using meta-analysis. The eight qualitative studies retrieved were synthesised using NVivo software (which is used for qualitative analysis) in a form of meta-synthesis. Thirdly the meta-analysis and the meta-synthesis were combined in order to identify aspects of the experimental studies that built on barriers and facilitators suggested by the children who had participated in the qualitative studies.

(Thomas et al., 2004)

Within a systematic review of studies of the effectiveness of an intervention, a synthesis of qualitative studies might be used to provide a greater theoretical understanding as to *why* an intervention might be effective, something which an experimental study cannot do. Undertaking separate syntheses of qualitative and experimental studies – addressing completely different research questions even though on the same topic area or field of practice – is increasingly becoming recognised as a powerful approach for understanding why interventions work (or not) as well as measuring the effect size of the intervention (if any). This is completely different from combining together in one synthesis studies across two or all three of the major types of research design outlined in this book. Such studies will address different primary research questions even if they are on the same topic area.

Research Summary

Mutual benefit of (separately) synthesising qualitative and experimental studies

This review focused on informal carers of people with dementia, who can suffer from depressive symptoms, emotional distress and other physiological, social and financial consequences. There were three main objectives.

1) *To produce a quantitative review of the efficacy of telephone counselling for informal carers of people with dementia.*
2) *To synthesise qualitative studies to explore carers' experiences of receiving telephone counselling and counsellors' experiences of conducting telephone counselling.*
3) *To integrate 1 and 2 to identify aspects of the intervention that are valued and work well, and those interventional components that should be improved or redesigned.*

Part One involved a meta-analysis of nine randomised controlled trials. Part Two involved a meta-synthesis of two qualitative studies. The authors' conclusion was that there is evidence that telephone counselling can reduce depressive symptoms for carers of people with dementia and that telephone counselling meets important needs of the carer. This result needs to be confirmed in future studies that evaluate efficacy through robust randomised controlled trials and the experience aspect through qualitative studies with rich data.

(Lins et al., 2014)

The value of a qualitative meta-synthesis in relation to social work interventions is that they can reveal some of the mechanisms that underpin 'successful' practice, and increase our understanding of the impact of needs and the mechanisms for the provision of services.

Becoming a social worker

Being able to synthesise research is a valuable skill for the professional social worker, not least because there is an increasing volume of research available. It is confusing if different messages arise from studies and are not reconciled with each other.

It is important that the profession develops the knowledge and skills in synthesising research so as to produce some reasonably agreed statement on our current state of knowledge on key questions. This chapter relates particularly to domain 5.10 of the PCF on recognising the contribution of research to inform practice and making use of research for this purpose.

Reflection Point

What use could you make in your practice of a robust synthesis of evidence?

Activity 8.3

Evidence into practice task

- Search a database to identify two or more papers reporting on research addressing what is essentially the same question and using the same method in terms of the major categories covered in this book.
- Having extracted data about the studies, undertake a narrative synthesis of the main findings of these papers.

Chapter Summary

- This chapter has outlined the distinction between the main types of synthesis of research and similar material.
- A narrative synthesis is where the results of studies, whether qualitative or quantitative, are combined into a narrative based on their main conclusions.
- A meta-synthesis is where the findings of qualitative studies are combined using principles of qualitative research.
- A meta-analysis is where the results of quantitative studies are combined quantitatively using explicit statistical principles.
- The principles of literature mapping have been outlined as a method to provide an overview of research across a broader topic.
- The main task undertaken by collaborators in the Cochrane and Campbell Collaborations in producing systematic reviews of the most robust studies of the effectiveness of social work interventions has been outlined.

Further Reading

Lipsey MW and Wilson DB (2001) *Practical Meta-Analysis*. Thousand Oaks, CA: SAGE.

This clear and concise book is recommended for the reader wanting to go to the next stage in developing skills in undertaking a meta-analysis.

Lundahl, B and Yaffe, J (2007) Use of meta-analysis in social work and allied disciplines. *Journal of Social Service Research,* 33 (3): 1–11.

This is a useful article on the place of meta-analysis in social work.

Popay, J, Roberts, H, Sowden, A, Petticrew, M, Arai, L, Rodgers, M, Britten, N, Roen, K and Duffy, S (2006) *Guidance on the Conduct of Narrative Synthesis in Systematic Reviews: A Product of the ESRC Methods Programme.* London: Economic and Social Research Council. Available at: www.lancaster. ac.uk/shm/research/nssr/research/dissemination/publications/NS_Synthesis_Guidance_v1.pdf

This guidance document includes pointers for narrative synthesis in the context of systematic approaches to study identification and appraisal.

Rutter, D, Francis, J, Coren, E and Fisher, M (2010) *SCIE Research Resource 1: SCIE Systematic Research Reviews: Guidelines* (2nd edition). London: Social Care Institute for Excellence. Available at: www.scie. org.uk/publications/researchresources/rr01.pdf

This SCIE guidance covers all stages of conducting a systematic review, for various types of research question and using differing types of synthesis as described in this chapter.

Sandelowski, M and Barroso, J (2007) *Handbook for Synthesising Qualitative Research.* New York: Springer.

This is one of the few books published that focuses on methods of synthesising qualitative research. It provides some useful pointers such as sensitivity to the context of the study and the theoretical constructs that shaped it.

Chapter 9

Getting research knowledge into practice within organisations

Introduction

Previous chapters in this book have set out the conceptual and theoretical arguments to support an evidence-informed framework based on a growing model of service delivery around the world. Such an approach has been adopted by a large number of professional bodies and is best described as a framework that makes use of current empirical evidence alongside professional judgement and the individual values and characteristics of clients. The status of registration as a professional social worker confers privilege and honour but equally it brings responsibilities. Individuals are legally accountable for their practice including the search for and use of evidence. Even if the organisational culture in which the individual is employed does not provide an environment conducive to research and evidence-informed practice, this does not absolve registered social workers from upholding registration standards. Chapter 2 has already articulated the roles and responsibilities of the individual professional in relation to evidence-informed practice. This chapter explores the wider organisational context in which evidence-informed practice is introduced. Arguably, the many features of an organisation such as culture, attitude, leadership, training and workforce opportunities, continuing professional development, governance and accountability, and social networks are all instrumental in either facilitating or inhibiting the use of research and evidence.

The primary focus of this chapter is a consideration of the opportunities that exist within and between organisations and their potential to facilitate social work professionals and teams in keeping up to date with evidence, and to feel confident about their knowledge base and begin to use research evidence to inform decisions. It commences with a brief overview of some of the barriers that inhibit adoption of evidence-based practice in social work. A number of local, national and international

129

perspectives are then used to illustrate developments that have taken place over the last couple of decades to improve the culture of research mindedness. In considering their impact, we contend that there is an urgent need to move beyond individual initiatives. Pivotal to the continual improvement of services for service users and carers is the need to develop a strategic vision with commitment from the leadership that creates and sustains an overarching organisational culture receptive to innovation and implementation of research and evidence in practice.

Barriers that exist in relation to research informing practice

Chapter 2 provided a detailed overview of the many barriers and impediments facing practitioners in fully embracing evidence-informed practice. Widescale consultative exercises conducted by the Institute for Research and Innovation in Social Services (IRISS, 2008) in Scotland and by the Centre for Social Work and Social Care Research, Swansea University (2009) in Wales confirmed the existence of such barriers. It is not the intention to repeat these here but rather to suggest that for some at least the validity of the claims may be less felt today. Given the rapid changes to research accessibility, emerging developments to information technology and the production of research synthesis, notably by both the Cochrane and Campbell Collaborations (discussed later in this chapter), access to compiled literature has increased substantially. Paradoxically, identifying relevant materials and evidence amid a world littered with an array of communication possibilities may be more complex and time-consuming for busy practitioners (Rowley and Johnson, 2013). See further discussion later in this chapter under the section on Cross-fertilisation of expertise and knowledge exchange hubs (pages 138–41).

Other barriers articulated in a literature review undertaken by IRISS (2008) relate to the wider organisational context in terms of culture and infrastructure. While these barriers are by no means unique to the social work profession, with education and nursing facing similar challenges, those relevant to social work include, for example:

- the organisational system is not always conducive to research and evidence utilisation;
- the infrastructure is weak;
- there is little articulation of social work and social care needs and priorities;
- there is limited training on research and critical appraisal; and
- research is not embedded within a research excellence framework.

A whole cultural shift is therefore necessary so that the vision ascribed to by both managers and practitioners – that service users and carers will benefit from social work being a more confident profession in the production and use of research and evidence to inform policy making and practice – can be fully realised.

As noted earlier, the focus of this chapter is on the range of initiatives and enablers that have the potential to support evidence-informed practice. Some of these already exist in the context of more organisational processes in the form of workforce requirement and regulatory frameworks and other wider workforce requirements. Other enablers are more specific, brought about by the deliberate creation of networks to help connect and exchange knowledge between organisations and more recently with those individuals who use services. The chapter considers a number of enablers under a number of selected areas:

- regulation of the workforce;

- continuing professional development;

- workforce development and training;

- informal learning approaches;

- cross-fertilisation of expertise and knowledge exchange hubs; and

- strategic direction and leadership.

Typology of implementation

Any discussion on getting research evidence and knowledge into social work practice organisations should consider the typology of implementation. A useful typology was articulated by Walter et al. (2004) and revised by Nutley (2010). In the three models outlined by these authors the term 'research' can easily be replaced by the term 'evidence'.

- The *research-based practitioner model*, which is most effective for the instrumental use of research by highly motivated and autonomous practitioners, making a linear use of research.

- The *embedded research model*, whereby it is assumed that evidence of what works becomes part of policy, guidelines and protocols.

- The *organisational excellence model*, which focuses at the macro level on creating research-minded cultures at a managerial level with an expectation of filtering down through the layers of the organisation to create a whole systems approach.

Nutley et al. (2009) suggest that the organisational excellence model is probably most important, but the least well developed, and in reality elements from all three are necessary. We will refer to the notion of excellence throughout this chapter.

Regulation of the workforce

Social work is practised in human service environments where research evidence is increasingly expected (Platt, 2014). Social workers work holistically with individuals and families, and with other professions in many diverse and often very complex social circumstances. These are circumstances where there are high levels of uncertainty, stress and risk, and often in situations where very often there are no clear answers. As articulated by the International Association of Schools of Social Work (2001) the social work profession promotes social change and problem solving in human relationships as well as the empowerment and liberation of people to enhance well-being. In addition, the principles of human rights and social justice, and personal and public involvement, are fundamental to social work. It is precisely these factors that have led to considerable dialogue and debate on the compatibility of the principles of an evidence-based approach with the principles, values and ethical base of the social work profession itself. This dialogue will undoubtedly continue. The need, however, for better and more robust research and evidence is now widely accepted and supported (Walter et al., 2004), and has been identified as a basic prerequisite for the professionalism of social work (Macdonald, 2003).

In debates about getting research and evidence into practice as a mainstream activity regulatory frameworks have immense potential to increase skill and confidence in undertaking research and evaluation activity, and applying evidence in practice. Opportunities exist within Care Council Regulations across the four councils of England, Wales, Scotland and Northern Ireland in their requirement placed on professionals to undertake their practice competently, keeping knowledge and skills up to date. In England, opportunities are also provided by the requirements of the Professional Capabilities Framework (PCF Capabilities 5 and 6) owned by The College of Social Work (TCSW, 2012). Likewise, a revised version of the National Occupational Standards, first developed in 2002, still applies in Scotland, Wales and Northern Ireland. These also place requirements on social workers to research, analyse, evaluate and use current knowledge of best social work practice.

Recognition and reward are also important factors when looking for opportunities to encourage greater ownership by professionals of the need to access and utilise research and evidence within their mainstream practice. As a regulated workforce, responsibilities of individual registrants and organisations for competence, conduct and keeping knowledge and skills up to date are made explicit within the various Codes of Practice of the Social Care Councils throughout the United Kingdom. A recent development in Northern Ireland is included here as an example as it shows promise for its contribution to getting research into practice.

Case Study 9.1

Professional in Practice Framework

Professional in Practice: The Continuous Professional Development Framework for Social Work is an initiative by the Northern Ireland Social Care Council (NISCC). It incorporates existing provision within the Post Qualifying (PQ) Framework. Existing PQ Awards and

Requirements, known as PiP Awards and Requirements, are worded specifically to encourage research-minded practice focusing on the understanding, demonstration and application of the following skills:

- critical judgement, critical reflection and critical analysis;
- analysis in applied research, professional research, audit and evaluation;
- conducting applied research, professional research, audit and evaluation.

These skills are taught and assessed within all approved programme provision, and submissions to the individual assessment route are assessed against these requirements.

An important factor in relation to this award process is that it moves beyond the approved educational programmes to also include recognition of smaller, practice-based professional developments that have the potential to both promote better use of research evidence and evaluation, and offer opportunities to work in partnership with service users and carers to collect and analyse their views.

Continuing professional development

During the last couple of decades there has been a growing recognition of the importance of evidence-based practice in social work education (JUCSWEC, 2006; Sheldon, 2001). This recognition has not been matched, however, by the provision of training to establish a sound foundation in social work evidence-based practice and research methodology. Some authors refer to a vicious circle of resistance to developing research capacity in social work whereby practitioners receive minimal research methods teaching at qualifying levels and few opportunities at post-qualifying level (Webber and Currin Salter, 2011). This position has created curricular challenges locally, nationally and internationally (Weissman and Sanderson, 2002). The future of evidence-informed practice in social work rests on the profession's capacity and willingness to provide current practitioners and future practitioners with training in evidence-based practice (Roberts and Yeaker, 2006). This also requires well-developed academic and agency partnership structures. Such structures, aimed at constructing the bridge between academia and practice, require both vision to develop and concerted effort to maintain. The benefits that emerge from such efforts through facilitated training opportunities for social work practitioners and managers at undergraduate, qualifying and post-qualifying levels are immense (Wilson and Douglas, 2007). With continuing professional development opportunities, staff are facilitated to acquire the necessary skills and knowledge for the application of research methods across the spectrum of research, evaluation and audit activities.

An example of a proactive partnership structure is outlined in Case Study 9.2. Of particular note in this discussion is the dual role that universities play in relation to social work research.

> ## Case Study 9.2
>
> ### University partnership and support for evidence-informed practice
>
> The two universities in Northern Ireland provide teaching and education to students, practitioners and managers at qualifying and post-qualifying levels, developing a culture of informed research mindedness and critical enquiry. Staff within the universities also undertake research across a range of topics and issues often in partnership with social work and social care organisations. A particular strength at the Social Work Departments is that all academic staff in social work posts must be on the professional social work register and subject to the same requirements for registration as social workers in practice.

The requirement for registration helps ensure that academic social work staff (both teaching and research) remain firmly rooted in professional practice, and issues are critically appraised using relevant methodologies underpinned by sound theoretical knowledge. Of particular importance are the opportunities that this offers for establishing and sustaining better linkages between research and practice (academia and practice), and in enhancing and supporting a strong culture of partnerships, communication and mutual learning in evidence-informed practice to investigate real-world practice issues (Haight, 2010). Such an approach is not without challenges, however, such as mistrust and lack of clarity in role definition and assignment. These need to be resolved to ensure that partnerships are constructive. Minkler and Wallerstein (2003) suggest that the one useful approach for resolution is that of community-based participatory research (CBPR) to support long-term mutual relationships between social workers, practitioners and academic researchers.

Workforce development and training

Leaders and managers play an essential role in facilitating research-minded practice through workforce development supports, including staff selection, induction and training. With current changes for innovation and learning within organisations, middle managers have a pivotal role in this regard. Recruitment processes, if designed for creativity and innovation, can provide immense potential to assist in developing overall organisational practice around practice research. Job descriptions could be redesigned to better reflect relevant research and evidence responsibilities aligned to organisational needs, as could more effective targeting of training and support provided.

Staff development and training strategies designed to promote research-minded practice can facilitate the overall research engagement and the critical reflexivity of practitioners. Harrison and Humphreys (1998) provide useful insights into the definition of the research-literate or research-minded practitioner from the perspective of the practitioner. For these authors a number of attributes are necessary: an attitude that is disposed towards seeking out new information; a capacity for critical reflection on practice in order to ask researchable questions; a capacity to be informed by research knowledge specifically related to social work values; and a capacity to understand research methodologies. It is not unreasonable to assume that academic pursuits at various levels of graduate and postgraduate study should equip practitioners to gain an overview of research methods and an appetite to undertake research-relevant projects. Austin et al. (2012) lament the fact, however, that a number of research methods courses are taught with limited attention to practice. Consequently, the level of appreciation of research and its relevance to day-to-day practice situations generally remains low.

When constructive relationships between academia and social work practice agencies have been fostered, positive results can emerge within the curriculum. Academic courses that have a direct relevance to social work practice can be created. Such programmes are unfortunately still perceived as relatively unique developments in the United Kingdom and internationally (JUCSWEC, 2006). Case Study 9.3, which details a specific programme, is included by way of illustrating good practice in this area.

Case Study 9.3

Research methods training course

The Application of Research Methods in Social Work was developed between the University of Ulster and the Health and Social Care Organisations in Northern Ireland. This introductory course in research methods was developed over two decades ago to address the need of professional social work practitioners, managers and trainers to develop skills in design, data collection, analysis and dissemination. Its objective was to help improve service quality and professional knowledge through research, professional audit and service evaluation. It was also to build the capacity and competence of social work practitioners to understand and undertake research and apply the evidence to practice. The value of this programme was its applicability to practice and its requirement for the conduct of a real-life practice project and the opportunity to disseminate the findings internally and externally through publication.

Opportunities to develop knowledge and skills in research, audit and evaluation for professional social workers have the potential for other positive outcomes such as a personal learning journey by practitioners in pursuit of academic awards at Master's or Ph.D. levels, or career development within management and academia.

Attending specialised research methods' training courses as part of post-qualifying learning and development is, of course, the pinnacle in the career trajectory of a research-minded practitioner. Its potential contribution to an overall shift in practice or culture remains low, however. A much longer-term, collaborative alignment of research and evidence into broader organisational workforce and training plans is necessary, as is an alignment of research and evidence with other mainstream activities. Supervision, for example, offers an ideal opportunity to discuss research evidence and its implications for practice, albeit that time constraints and case-load pressures may pose challenges. The valuable space that supervision offers to reflect on learning and research as part of professional development should be fully grasped.

With the growing paradigm shift towards the need for evidence-based practice (Mathieson and Hohman, 2013), cognisance also needs to be taken of the literature that suggests that qualifying students, despite having access to a greater wealth of information than previous generations of students and practitioners, do not develop the skills through their training to be able to access and analyse critically the research which might inform practice (Howard et al., 2003). Investment will be required to ensure that future generations of social workers, and those already in practice, are provided with knowledge in evidence-based practice, inclusive of highly tuned investigative and appraisal skills, and skills in literature search. This activity demands intelligence and imagination particularly in the area of evidence synthesis and its application to practice and service delivery.

Case Study 9.4, drawn from Northern Ireland, describes and outlines the rationale of a recent development in this regard.

Case Study 9.4

The Evidence-Informed Practice and Organisation training module

The Evidence-Informed Practice and Organisation training module is in the early stages of development in 2015. It aims to equip professional social workers employed as practitioners, managers, trainers and regulators in health and social services, criminal justice, education welfare and voluntary sector social care organisations with the knowledge and skills to identify, appraise, synthesise and disseminate research and other evidence to inform social work practice in their own setting. The module aims to support the development and maintenance of high quality social work and social care services. A requirement will be placed on participants to develop a review proposal; conduct the review, involving identifying relevant research and other knowledge from databases and other sources, appraising quality and synthesising; submitting a review report (dissertation); and undertaking a presentation in their own organisation based on this review.

The value of such a module is that it is responding to changing and more immediate demands of the health and social care organisations rather than being academically driven. It will be practice based, and will address and inform issues arising directly from the practice experience of the participants. An additional and important feature is that the programme aims to support candidates to demonstrate competence in professional social work that meets the requirements of the Northern Ireland Post Qualifying Education and Training Partnership.

Informal learning approaches

The identification, evaluation and integration of multiple sources of knowledge and evidence require critical thinking and reflection augmented by creativity and curiosity (TCSW, 2012). An understanding of the contribution of research evidence and its application is a key component within this diverse mix of knowledge but it remains one of the most challenging for practitioners. In the midst of busy workloads when attendance at training can be perceived by colleagues as an added luxury, rather than an essential component of good practice, such a challenge needs to be addressed through the development and support of an imaginative mix of other initiatives.

It often falls to the workplace and 'on the job' training for practitioners to value the use of research and see the benefits within a wider organisational context (Austin et al., 2012). For practitioners pre-disposed to critical reflection and curiosity the evidence-informed demands being placed on organisations to pay more attention to measuring and assessing outcomes have provided a welcome opportunity to look for new ways of working and reflecting on practice. Austin et al. (2012) suggest that there are numerous approaches, some of which include the simplest methods of fostering learning – for example, the scheduling of regular staff development events in the form of journal clubs; in-house learning events such as lunchtime seminars and presentations; and the establishment of communities of practice around practice issues. Management support that allows staff the time and the resource to search out the literature, review it, share and discuss the outcomes and review the learning with colleagues, and all in a safe place to unpack service issues, remains an invaluable approach.

The tangible benefits drawn from one such practice example through the establishment of a journal club are outlined in Case Study 9.5.

Case Study 9.5

A journal club used for team development

A period of transition within a Dementia Home Support Team in one social work organisation provided an opportunity for staff to seek out new evidence to help guide them on the best way forward when providing behavioural assessment and intervention within the individual home setting. Previously assessments were provided by the team only in care home settings. Searches were carried out on electronic databases, namely, MEDLINE and PsycINFO. Articles were shared among the team and each team member was responsible for presenting an article. Each team member was tasked with summarising two or three points of key learning that could influence the development of the team.

(Harvey, 2014)

The key learning from this work was the opportunity it generated in the active involvement of the whole team in influencing service development. This meant that the workload was shared evenly; and the findings influenced the development of the team resulting in a transfer of ideas to other services to support individuals with dementia.

The size and scale of such initiatives is not necessarily the issue. While the example quoted above was relatively small scale, it resulted in a number of other spin-offs. One very positive outcome was the generation of staff enthusiasm, and in particular their ongoing enthusiasm to continue to learn from literature and actively use research to help find solutions to the challenges encountered. This is an essential element of evidence-informed practice. With management support that offers space and time to develop, small initiatives have the potential to progress from 'mini acorns to mighty oaks'. The journal club, in this instance, has evolved from a necessary practice exercise completed at an in-service development day to a regular quarterly event. Work remains incremental with opportunities now being provided to staff to learn about electronic database searching.

Where staff are privileged also to have access to technological support, the benefits accrued are immense. Within the regional health and social care services in Northern Ireland, Health on the Net Northern Ireland – commonly known as HONNI – is available to each member of staff on their computer, thus facilitating automatic access to a wide range of electronic databases and resources. Initiatives such as this remain important and instrumental in generating and maintaining an appetite for seeking out and using research evidence to inform service provision.

Time spent on research and participation activity also needs to be valued by the organisation as an integral element of service improvement and staff development. The corollary to the journal club example is when staff are encouraged to actively pursue practitioner research but where no protected time is provided. In such circumstances pressures from their casework and emergency work will inevitably predominate. Such models will be less likely to succeed when full managerial commitment is lacking.

Cross-fertilisation of expertise and knowledge exchange hubs

Human decisions are generally thought to be based on the present evidence and a rational decision process. For professionals, the key is to make the knowledge base and decision process explicit for other purposes such as accountability, reflective learning and teaching skills to others. For social workers, this demand for more explicit decision making relates particularly to such contexts as interprofessional case conferences in complex care situations, and contested court hearings in relation to child protection. The emerging world of evidence-based practice is concerned with explicit use of the best available knowledge to inform decisions and therefore requires greater cross-fertilisation of expertise and the sharing of knowledge.

Over a number of decades a variety of networks, best described as knowledge-exchange networks, have been established locally, nationally and internationally aimed at providing organisations with a broader pool of relevant and complementary knowledge. A number of these are explored in this chapter by way of illustration rather than a comprehensive list. All can be classified as forms of knowledge exchange networks and hubs. If, however, potential users are to gain most benefit from their use, it is important to have a clear understanding of their respective features such as accessibility, genesis, intent and the rigour adopted in compiling content. It is also important to be clear for what purpose the network and information are required. Some networks are intended to provide easy access to organisational knowledge and information about publications, events and good practice; other organisations aim to provide best available evidence using rigorous methodology and approaches, whereas others are concerned with the production of systematic reviews, which are often referred to as the gold standard in evidence synthesis.

Table 9.1 summarises the contribution of a number of these networks and provides additional comment on their value and contribution in the transfer of knowledge into organisations.

Table 9.1 Knowledge exchange networks

Name	Scope	Comments
HSC Knowledge Exchange	The Knowledge Exchange is a resource for people delivering Health and Social Care in Northern Ireland. It provides space (online, by phone and in person) for staff to meet, discuss, debate and tackle emerging and current trends in health and social care. It provides access to resources, good practice, leading thinking and up-to-date news and events across local, national and international systems.	A local resource for staff to access and provide organisational information. Categorisation is by case studies, publications, videos, audio tools and apps, presentations and research. Issues of rigour not prioritised. It is a place where staff can upload and showcase their work for the benefit of others. Useful for front-line staff and managers alike. No subscription fee.
Social Care Institute for Excellence (SCIE)	SCIE disseminates knowledge-based guidance; involves people who use services, carers, practitioners, providers and policy makers in advancing and promoting good practice in social care and enhancing the skills and professionalism of social care workers through tailored, targeted and user-friendly resources. It covers England, Wales and Northern Ireland.	Materials are innovative and customer focused. Rigour and accessibility to information are priorities. Evidence is rooted to practice; collaboration and co-production are main methods of working. Useful for front-line staff, managers, commissioners and policy makers. Membership based but no subscription fee.

(Continued)

Table 9.1   Continued

Name	Scope	Comments
RiP (Research in Practice for Children) and RiPfA (Research in Practice for Adults)	RiP and RiPfA are national agencies based in Dartington that produce accessible online resources similar to SCIE (see above) but they have a greater focus on how these resources are used in practice. In addition to providing hard copy and web-based resources for subscribing local authorities they also provide sector-led support in the form of national workshops, conferences, webinars and knowledge exchange events. Tailored support is provided as 20 hours per year, one-to-one support, reason-evaluation service, and action research-based change projects.	Attention to accessibility but with a greater focus on practice application. A limited amount of material is available free of charge but access to resources requires an annual subscription fee.
IRISS (Institute for Research and Innovation in Social Services)	IRISS is a charitable company which aims to promote positive outcomes for the people who use Scotland's social services. It achieves this by enhancing the capacity and capability of the social services workforce to access and make use of knowledge and research for service innovation and improvement through three programmes: Evidence-informed Practice; Innovation; and Improvement and Knowledge Media.	Attention to accessibility. Valuable resources for innovation and improvement. Less engaged in the generation of new research evidence. There is no subscription fee. Offers online access to thousands of resources.
Practice and Research Together (PART), Canada	PART was founded in 2006 in Ontario. The core function is to distil and disseminate practice-relevant research findings to child welfare practitioners. It works in close partnership with RiP (see above), with whom it shares resources. It has a simple and very accessible website which enables navigation to its range of resources and activities.	Attention to research utilisation. Access to network is via a membership subscription fee. Easy navigation.
SAaRIH (Safeguarding Adults at Risk Information Hub), sga@RIHM	The SAaRIH Project is an online central information resource for practitioners, managers, researchers, educators and policy makers (across all relevant disciplines and agencies and sectors) with an interest in adult safeguarding and protection.	Attention to accessibility of the material through a well-designed categorisation system by type of knowledge. Access to published research in peer-reviewed journals. Access is via a subscription fee by organisation.
Campbell Collaboration	The Campbell Collaboration is an international research network that produces systematic reviews of the effects of social interventions. Campbell is based on voluntary co-operation among researchers from a variety of backgrounds.	Provides robust evidence at policy and strategic levels. Rigour and robustness of the evidence is a priority. More information is available in the Further Reading in Chapters 1 and 4.
Cochrane Collaboration	The Cochrane Collaboration helps policy makers, providers, service recipients, their advocates and carers make well-informed decisions about health and care. They do this by preparing, updating and promoting over 5,000 reviews and maintaining the largest record of randomised controlled trials in the world.	Provides robust evidence at policy and strategic levels. Rigour and robustness of evidence is a priority. More information is available in the Further Reading in Chapters 1 and 4.
DARES (Decisions, Assessment, Risk and Evidence Studies in Social Work)	This research cluster undertakes research, teaching and organisational development to support social work and allied human service professions in four areas: professional judgement and shared decision making; assessment processes and tools to inform decisions; risk assessment and management in practice and organisations; and creating and using evidence to inform practice and policy.	Networking opportunities are provided through DARES events. These reflect a healthy cross-fertilisation of expertise and sharing of knowledge from academia and practice – researcher to practitioner; and practitioner to researcher.

Name	Scope	Comments
DARE IV	This research cluster is responsible for hosting a series of international biennial symposiums on Decisions, Assessment, Risk and Evidence in Social Work – the next symposium, DARE IV, is planned for 2016.	Provides networking opportunities for managers, practitioners, policy makers and academics to engage in debate and dialogue with expert inputs from renowned national and international speakers. Financial support provided by the local commissioner for health and social care facilitates practitioner attendance and recognises the contribution of this less traditional and formalised form of learning.
Better Care Exchange	Online space for sharing learning, information and good practice on delivering integrated health and social care. Built on a collaboration approach across sectors.	Useful resource that operates as a learning hub through an online network with peers. The emphasis is on linking professionals working in integrated health and social care. It is a social media site for sharing good practice Free access to over 400 resources, videos and links to leading organisations. Less attention to rigour.

Strategic direction and leadership

For decades it has been agreed that strong leadership, an organisational need and a supportive management structure form the essential requirements for developing and expanding the social work research capacity (Walter et al., 2004). Strong leadership at all levels within an organisation embodies and models the key principles of a learning organisation. Leaders have the potential to influence the development of the culture and therefore are instrumental in creating such an organisation receptive to creativity, innovation and new ideas.

Throughout this chapter a range and variety of initiatives has been discussed in the context of the valuable contribution that they each make in beginning to develop the research orientation of an organisation's culture and in pursuing learning and excellence. In the context of the excellence model as outlined by Walter et al. (2004) and Nutley et al. (2009), it is evident that individually these initiatives fall short of what was intended. In this chapter we now move the debate a step further to consider the potential contribution of setting a strategic vision with visible commitment from leadership to support excellence and capacity in this area.

Throughout the United Kingdom there has been a vast array of research and evidence-informed strategies developed, all aimed at giving a strategic lead within respective organisations. The Economic and Social Research Council (ESRC) is the primary United Kingdom funder of long-term strategic social science research. It is particularly concerned with identifying societal issues, coordinating research capacity and ensuring a continuous supply of skilled people to address these issues in the future.

Annual plans for delivery are developed to support a portfolio of activities aimed at supporting excellence. The Welsh Government's National Institute for Social Care and Health Research is notable for the position that the Welsh government affords social care research, placing it on an equal footing to that of health. This articulates a positive strategic message to social work in Wales. The strategy had as its intent the provision of funding of an infrastructure to support excellence in health and social care research and development activity.

Specifically in relation to Higher Education in the United Kingdom, the Joint University Council Social Work Education Committee (JUCSWEC, 2006) was instrumental in recognising the importance that good quality research and evidence can make to the lives of the millions of people who come into contact with social workers and social care services. Its particular aim was to:

- maximise the Higher Education Institutes' contribution to social work and social care service improvement;
- develop a strong evidence base for social work and social care services; and
- build a workforce capable of using evidence critically and effectively.

In Northern Ireland, the *Social Work Research and Continuous Improvement Strategy 2015–2020* (HSCB, 2015) was designed specifically to support the promotion of a culture of evidence-informed practice, quality, service and user outcomes, and the delivery of research, evaluation and audit across social work services.

While all of these strategies are designed in different contexts there are a number of key and similar features. These include:

- a nominated senior leader to drive forward;
- a steering group to keep on track;
- a vision of what research and evidence-informed practice looks like;
- a strategic plan, with key priorities, about how to get there;
- a coherent strategic planning process; and
- a monitoring and review process.

To make the strategic difference as intended by the strategies, a number of key dimensions also need to be addressed, including:

- resources;
- infrastructure;
- capacity and capability;
- visibility and impact; and
- governance.

The overlapping commitment of any of the aforenamed strategies was the desire to raise the quality and the quantity of research, evidence and its use. This is based on the premise that driving the research and evidence-based agenda forward can make a difference to the lives of people who come into contact with social work services (JUCSWEC, 2006). In a rapidly changing social and economic landscape, social work research has the potential to contribute to a whole range of new and emerging evidence needs in relation to the demography, personalisation, choice, inclusion, safety, autonomy, partnerships, personal and public involvement (service users and carer involvement), equality and human rights. Setting a strategic vision in relation to research and translating that vision into reality is therefore crucial (see Figure 9.1).

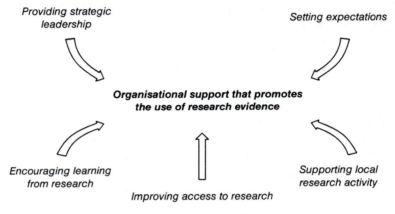

Providing strategic leadership

Setting expectations

Organisational support that promotes the use of research evidence

Encouraging learning from research

Supporting local research activity

Improving access to research

Figure 9.1 Organisational supports that promote the use of evidence

Adapted from Atherton and Hodson (2006)

Strategic priorities and an associated framework for practice can set out an exciting, albeit challenging agenda. It is, however, a relatively well-accepted fact that any strategy will only ever be as good as its execution. The energy and drive that go into strategy formulation need to be matched, threefold at least, in the implementation phase. In the example quoted above in relation to Northern Ireland, it is acknowledged that this is very much a step change and that sustained effort and drive over the years will be required if the full potential in building a body of research and evidence, and of supporting better linkages and accessibility of research to practice and practice to research, is to be realised.

In developing a strategy it is always helpful at an early stage to also begin considering what success factors would look like. This approach helps generate thinking on expectations and intended outcomes and if these are articulated consistently throughout all communications and engagement processes, alongside key actions, the strategic vision is more likely to become a reality. Figure 9.2 provides some suggestions on possible success factors associated with the development of a social work research strategy. The success factors are multidimensional but can be summarised into seven key areas relevant to work of this nature.

- The establishment of a mechanism to determine and review research priorities that are driven and owned by the sector itself linked to funding.
- The development of an active research culture that promotes the importance of robust research evidence.
- Greater collaboration between academic and other research providers and practice settings in order to foster reciprocal relationships and partnership working to identify and fill existing evidence gaps.
- Work that helps understand and tackle the barriers to evidence-informed practice.
- An increase in the exchange, dissemination and use of research and evidence that is accessible to those who need to use it.
- Better engagement and involvement of service users in the whole research process.
- Greater attention to how to define and measure outcomes of social work and social care interventions and services.

Figure 9.2 Success factors associated with research and evidence strategies (HSCB, 2015)

Strategies need active engagement of interested stakeholders. Once drafted, the strategy needs to be consulted upon to seek wider views and opinions, and suggestions for refinements. This is a key step in the strategy formulation as it articulates widely the internal commitment of the organisation and helps build momentum and wider ownership. It also helps in sending out a clear message from the social work leadership to other professions, not about articulating the need to have a distinct research strategy for social work, but rather about having a strategy that highlights the necessary place of research and evidence in helping to demonstrate the distinctive quality of the social work profession and providing a strategic way forward to achieve this.

Becoming a social worker

Individual practitioners remain responsible for keeping their knowledge and skills up to date and promoting the centrality of evidence-informed practice. They should understand and apply knowledge to their practice and have an understanding of social work through both evidence gathering and research.

Reflection Point

There are a number of organisational barriers that exist but we are on a journey, and by better understanding and embracing these challenges we will move further in our journey to increase the quantity and quality of evidence-informed practice in social work. Can you identify the type of organisational supports that already exist within your organisation that you consider help implement research and evidence?

Activity 9.1

Evidence into practice task

- Identify at least three things you will do to ensure that you are taking full advantage of these supports in order to make a personal contribution to the wider cultural shift of evidence-informed practice.
- Develop a creative approach to share the outcomes with your colleagues.

Chapter Summary

- Social work professionals face many barriers and impediments in fully embracing evidence-informed practice.
- There are a number of barriers that relate to the wider organisational context in terms of the overall culture and infrastructure. The specifics include, for example, that the organisation is not always conducive to research and evidence utilisation; the infrastructure is weak; there is little articulation of social work and social care needs and priorities; there is limited training on research and critical appraisal; and research is not embedded within a research excellence framework.
- A range of opportunities already exist within and between organisations that have the potential to support social work professionals and teams in keeping up to date with evidence, feeling confident about their knowledge base and beginning to use research evidence to inform decisions.
- While individually many initiatives have an important role to play in shifting the debate on evidence-informed social work practice, policy and commissioning, none has achieved the desired level required.
- There are a number of promising examples emerging in the form of research strategies that relate specifically to social work research and evidence. These strategies demonstrate leadership and commitment, and offer immense potential to shift the culture and help secure the mainstreamed implementation of research and evidence in practice.
- Concerted and sustainable effort is required in the implementation of these strategies so that the vision articulated is fully achieved.
- Even with organisational commitment, the process of getting robust evidence into practice is not an easy one. A number of barriers will continue to exist but we are on a journey and by better understanding and embracing these challenges we will move further in our journey towards increasing the quantity and quality of evidence-informed practice in social work.

Further Reading

National Institute for Health Research (2010) *Systematic Reviews: Knowledge to support evidence-informed health and social care.* London: NIHR. Available at: www.nihr.ac.uk/documents/about-NIHR/NIHR-Publications/NIHR-Systematic-Reviews-Infrastructure.pdf

This NIHR document provides very clear guidance on major sources of systematic reviews and contacts in the field.

National Research Ethics Service (2013) *Defining Research.* London: Health Research Authority. Available at: www.hra.nhs.uk/documents/2013/09/defining-research.pdf

This short document helpfully provides authoritative guidance on the distinction between 'research', 'service evaluation' and 'professional audit' for governance purposes. It is most easily found by using a search engine to search for 'defining research'.

Soydan, H and Palinkas, L (2014) *Evidence-based Practice in Social Work: Development of a new professional culture.* London: Routledge.

This book contains a useful discussion that moves our thinking beyond the individual perspective of evidence-informed practice, an aspect that predominates the literature, to an exploration of the organisational perspective. It draws on a number of efforts and strategies underway to build leadership, collaboration and sustainability.

Taylor, BJ and Campbell, B (2011) Quality, risk and governance: Social workers' perspectives. *International Journal of Leadership in Public Services,* 7(4): 256–72.

This article outlines a broad conceptual framework for considering quality in social care organisations, including the place of knowledge from research to informed practice and policy.

Chapter 10

Conclusion

The journey so far

This book aims to enable readers to develop the knowledge and skills necessary for identifying, appraising and synthesising research. The topic relates to fundamental social work knowledge and skill areas such as recognising the contribution of research to developing practice; being able to keep up to date with newly published research; making use of research to improve practice; and demonstrating an understanding of research methods. The book has been mapped to the Professional Capabilities Framework for Social Workers in England, and relates more broadly to Higher Education Quality Assurance Standards and professional post-qualifying frameworks in other jurisdictions.

Reflective practice is an essential professional practice skill, enabling learning and transfer of knowledge across situations and contexts. However, reflecting on your practice in a vacuum can be unproductive in terms of learning. Reflection needs to connect insight into practice with sound research and useful theory to be most effective. The role of this book is to support continuing professional reflective practice by facilitating the connection with useful, relevant, high quality knowledge rooted in sound research.

Knowledge creation is a cyclic, cumulative process. It requires both inductive (typically qualitative) research and deductive (typically experimental) research to complement each other. Inductive research provides new insights, raises new questions and provides new conceptualisations and theoretical understandings of issues. Deductive research measures such conceptualisations and theoretical constructs to see if they hold true in the real world. Experimental studies measure whether interventions work or not; qualitative research helps us understand why they work (or not).

It is essential that professionals grasp the distinction between different types of research questions, and the research designs most suited to addressing those questions. That is a major issue addressed by this book. A second major component of the book is to teach the detailed knowledge and skills required to locate research. In this digital age the opportunities are mushrooming; we need to keep abreast of them. A third development in this book has been to create a suite of appraisal tools for surveys and qualitative and (quasi-)experimental studies. We did not venture into this without some trepidation, knowing that there are so many appraisal tools already in existence. Two of the major triggers were, first, that the renowned CASP series does not include a tool for appraising surveys and, second, that we did not find the existing tools sufficiently well suited to the social workers we teach. The readers and our future students will no doubt give us feedback on the success of this venture. Comments for improvement welcome!

Another area where this book is original is in addressing the 'evidence challenge' to organisations as well as to individual professionals as complementary aspects of the challenge to the profession. Particularly in large, taxpayer-funded social care systems as exist in most democratic countries, the responsibility for evidence-informed practice lies with organisations as well as with individuals. Employers, and those who commission and contract services, have governance responsibilities to ensure that practice is sound. Such endeavours will be limiting and limited if they are restricted to monitoring service quality. Leadership must be exercised in developing a research-informed culture. The developing digital age means that learning must be seen in a context beyond individual training courses. As the potential mechanisms for transfer of knowledge grow, organisations will need to decide on systems in which to invest resources so as to inform best practice and promote an effective learning culture that includes an understanding and use of research.

This book is firmly located in what we understand to be sound and ethical principles of evidence-based or evidence-informed practice. Using interventions with disregard for evidence that they are ineffective is immoral. Failing to seek the best evidence to inform judgements and interventions is not acceptable for any professional. However, this does not mean that we relegate study designs other than experimental ones to a lesser place within the whole endeavour to create knowledge, as we hope is apparent from the text. Our tenet is that the design must match the type of research question primarily, as well as then taking into account ethical and practical issues as to what is feasible.

Even in relation to measuring effectiveness of interventions we are aware of the limitations of experimental studies in particular contexts. The state of professional knowledge on the topic is one aspect of deciding on the acceptability of undertaking an experimental study of effectiveness with its implications for resources and participants. Incidence may be low in a domain such as personal safety of staff (Taylor, 2011) so that even if randomisation to a new personal safety regime were possible, statistical significance would be hard to achieve. For the sake of a broader education, the reader is recommended to read Smith and Pell (2003) who conducted a systematic review of randomised controlled trials of the use of parachutes. Unsurprisingly, they were not able to identify any randomised trials but note that their safety is well-enough attested by observational studies. Nonetheless, in our own field the social work profession must face the challenges in undertaking high quality experimental studies if we are to demonstrate effectiveness of our interventions. Avoidance behaviours in relation to experimental studies are rarely as justifiable as in the case of parachute interventions. It is only through a broad approach that recognises stages of building an intervention based on best evidence (Medical Research Council, 2008) that we can create a robust knowledge base of which interventions are more likely to be effective for particular problems in particular circumstances.

Identifying relevant research and appraising its quality are two major steps in developing an approach to practice based on best evidence. The third is to synthesise the best, relevant research in a way that directly addresses a professional issue, whether practice, management, teaching or regulation. The objective that we set ourselves regarding this is that readers should be able to carry out a narrative synthesis, and understand the essentials of meta-analysis and meta-synthesis when they encounter these and to prepare the way for those who go on to Ph.D. study and systematic reviews. Methods for the synthesis stage are less well developed than for study identification and appraisal. We look forward to seeing an increasing number of syntheses by social workers and methodological developments which we can report in the next edition.

The importance of knowledge for individual practitioners and for organisations that employ social workers cannot be over-emphasised. This book has focused consciously on practical steps that social work professionals and organisations can undertake to develop their use of research so as to improve services. Nonetheless, we recognise, of course, the many challenges that face any profession – and social work in particular – in developing the creation and use of research. Perhaps the biggest challenge that we face is the fear among any social workers who conceive of their work as shrouded in a mystique that is beyond discussion, beyond rational justification and beyond the understanding of anyone outside the profession. Such an approach will be strongly challenged by an evidence-based practice approach which seeks rational debate about the nature of social problems and the forms of intervention that are found to be helpful.

Further developments

The profession of social work needs to invest energy and skills in the development of a sound knowledge base. This applies to individual professionals and to the employers of social workers. It is reasonable that taxpayers and charity-donors expect that their money is used effectively. This does not mean that every client will be helped or that every tragedy will be averted any more than anyone using a headache tablet with proven effectiveness will always have their headache relieved. However, it does mean that over time and over a number of clients and contexts, we can demonstrate that our efforts are having a positive effect.

For the profession we hope that this book has highlighted scope for continuing development of 'the knowledge base to create a knowledge base'. In particular, we would like to see progress in areas such as:

- improvement in database provision for the social work profession;

- professional consensus on a (gradually evolving) thesaurus of terms which would make study identification more straightforward;

- development and refinement of 'search strings' for common social work topics;

- increased use and standardisation of tables of key data from studies;

- continuing development of study appraisal in relation to drawing a threshold for inclusion, the threshold depending on the topic and rigour for the review;

- greater involvement in meta-analysis of (quasi-)experimental studies of effectiveness, including through the Cochrane and Campbell Collaborations;

- development of meta-synthesis of qualitative studies across types of qualitative research;

- careful and insightful narrative synthesis using various frames of reference so as to provide a balanced overview of research that will inform practice and policy; and

- the development of creative organisational approaches to knowledge transfer so that the ever-increasing knowledge base reaches front-line professionals.

The challenge addressed by this book is one that needs to be taken up by every social worker and by every employer of social workers. All professionals need to be able to understand and use research even though each profession needs only a few people skilled in managing a research project in all its detail. However, during the course of their career all social workers should expect to be involved in research in some way, just as they should expect to contribute at some stage in a leadership capacity and in training others. We hope that this book will enable all social workers – in any setting whether practice, policy, management, training or regulation – to be more skilled in understanding and using research. We also hope that it will inspire some social workers to continue their career journey towards greater involvement in designing and carrying out research.

The 'knowledge explosion' is here to stay. The information age brought about by the digital revolution means not only that there are now more opportunities open to us, but also that society's expectations of us are greater. We can do no more than respond as best we can to ensure that we use the best available evidence to inform our practice, for the ultimate benefit of our clients and their families.

Appendix 1

QAT-S: Quality Appraisal Tool: Survey research

1. Is the rationale for the study adequately described?

   a. Does the study have a clearly formulated question, aims and objectives?

   b. Was the question developed from a review of existing research and theory?

2. Is the study design appropriate?

   a. Is there an explicit and valid rationale for the chosen method of administration (e.g. telephone interview, online or postal questionnaire, email distribution, etc.)?

   b. Is the method of administration identical for all cases?

   c. Has the potential for bias been addressed?

3. Is the sampling strategy clearly defined and justified?

   a. Has the method of sampling (subjects and setting) been clearly described?

   b. Is the sampling frame representative of the population?

   c. Was the necessary sample size calculated?

   d. Was the response rate adequate?

4. Are ethical issues adequately addressed?

   a. Was research ethics approval sought and obtained?

   b. Has consultation with service users and practitioners been discussed?

   c. Are issues of informed consent and confidentiality discussed satisfactorily?

   d. Were sponsorship and conflicts of interest considered?

5. Is the method for data collection appropriate?

   a. Was the development of the data collection tool described in sufficient detail?

   b. Was the method of data collection piloted?

   c. Has the validity and reliability of the data collection tool been discussed?

6. Are the methods used for analysing data appropriate?

   a. Was the approach to data analysis clearly described?

   b. Was the method of analysis justified?

   c. Was the testing of the statistical significance of any correlations appropriate?

7. Are the research findings adequately presented?

   a. Are the findings presented in a manner that is clear and understandable?

   b. Have the main characteristics of the participants been described?

   c. Do the findings summarise all the data gathered?

   d. Is there discussion of any null or negative outcomes?

8. Are the research findings credible?

   a. Do the findings address the research question?

   b. Are limitations of the study discussed?

   c. Are non-respondents and missing data accounted for?

9. Are the discussion and conclusions justified and appropriate?

   a. Are the findings discussed in the light of existing literature?

   b. Are conclusions justified by the findings?

   c. Have alternative explanations for the findings been explored and discounted?

   d. Have interaction effects and confounding factors been considered?

10. To what extent are the findings of the study transferable to other settings?

   a. Were the subjects similar in important respects to those of interest to you?

   b. Was the context similar to or different from your own setting?

   c. How applicable are the findings to practice, policy or theoretical knowledge?

Appendix 2

QAT-Q: Quality Appraisal Tool: Qualitative studies

1. Is the rationale for the study adequately described?

    a. Does the study have a clearly formulated question, aims and objectives?

    b. Was the question developed from a review of existing research and theory?

2. Is the method of conducting the study appropriate?

    a. Is there an explicit and valid rationale for the chosen method (grounded theory, interpretative phenomenological analysis, discourse analysis, etc.)?

    b. Is there an explicit and valid rationale for the chosen method of data gathering (focus groups, interviews, observation, etc.)?

3. Is the sampling strategy clearly defined and justified?

    a. Has the method of sampling (subjects and setting) been clearly described?

    b. Have the main characteristics of the participants been described?

    c. Is the sample information-rich in relation to the study topic?

    d. Is there a discussion about saturation of data?

4. Are ethical issues adequately addressed?

    a. Was research ethics approval sought and obtained?

    b. Has consultation with service users and practitioners been discussed?

    c. Are issues of informed consent and confidentiality discussed satisfactorily?

    d. Were sponsorship and conflicts of interest considered?

    e. Has the researcher reflected on his or her own role and potential bias?

5. Is the method for data collection appropriate?

    a. Was the development of the aide-memoire for data collection justified?

    b. Was the aide-memoire for data collection piloted?

    c. Has the learning from the piloting been recorded?

6. Is the method used for analysing data appropriate?

    a. Was the approach to data analysis clearly described?

    b. Was the method of analysis justified?

    c. How were themes derived and differences of interpretation resolved?

7. Are the research findings adequately presented?

    a. Are the findings presented in a manner that is clear and understandable?

    b. Are the findings evidenced adequately by direct quotations or observations?

    c. Do the findings provide a coherent model or conceptualisation on the topic?

    d. Is there discussion of any more extreme or contradictory responses?

8. Are the research findings credible?

    a. Do the findings address the research question?

    b. Are limitations of the study discussed?

    c. Is the data available for inspection beyond the primary researcher(s)?

    d. Did more than one researcher perform the analysis?

    e. Is data presented from a range of respondents or circumstances?

    f. Are the explanations (models) presented plausible and coherent?

9. Are the discussion and conclusions justified and appropriate?

    a. Are conclusions justified by the findings?

    b. Are the findings discussed in the light of previous research?

    c. Have alternative explanations for the findings been explored and discounted?

10. To what extent are the findings of the study transferable to other settings?

    a. Were the subjects similar in important respects to those of interest to you?

    b. Was the context similar to or different from your own setting?

    c. How applicable are the findings to practice, policy or theoretical knowledge?

Appendix 3

QAT-E: Quality Appraisal Tool: (Quasi-)Experimental studies

1. Is the rationale for the study adequately described?

   a. Does the study have a clearly formulated question, aims and objectives?

   b. Was the question developed from a review of existing research and theory?

2. Is the study design appropriate?

   a. Is there an explicit and valid rationale for the study design?

   b. Does the study have a clearly formulated design (e.g. natural experiment, (cluster) randomised, interrupted time series, case control study, pre-post testing, etc.)?

   c. What measures were taken to ensure fidelity (consistency) of the intervention?

   d. Does the control group receive standard treatment, no treatment, or an alternative intervention?

   e. Have threats to validity been adequately addressed (such as contemporaneous events, passage of time (maturation), regression to the mean)?

3. Is the sampling strategy clearly defined and justified?

   a. Has the method of sampling (subjects and setting) been clearly described?

   b. Have the main characteristics of the participants been described?

   c. Was the necessary sample size calculated?

   d. Are the intervention and control groups similar at the start?

   e. If randomised, how and was allocation concealed from participants (selection bias)?

   f. Are all those entering the study accounted for at the end (attrition)?

   g. Is there a discussion about recruitment and any refusal to participate?

4. Are ethical issues adequately addressed?

   a. Was research ethics approval sought and obtained?

   b. Has consultation with service users and practitioners been discussed?

  c. Are issues of informed consent and confidentiality discussed satisfactorily?

  d. Were sponsorship and conflicts of interest considered?

  e. Where randomised, have ethical issues been discussed?

5. Are the method for data collection appropriate?

  a. Are the sensitivity, validity and reliability of data collection tool(s) discussed?

  b. If a study with a control group, did those doing the measurements know to which group participants belonged (detection bias)?

6. Is the method used for analysing data appropriate?

  a. Was the approach to data analysis clearly described?

  b. Was the method of analysis justified?

  c. Was the testing of the statistical significance appropriate?

7. Are the research findings adequately presented?

  a. Are the findings presented in a manner that is clear and understandable?

  b. Do the findings summarise all the data gathered?

  c. Is there discussion of any null or negative outcomes?

8. Are the research findings credible?

  a. Do the findings address the research question?

  b. Are limitations of the study discussed?

  c. Is the approach to dealing with attrition and trial crossover justifiable?

  d. Are effects of contemporaneous events and passage of time considered?

9. Are the discussion and conclusions justified and appropriate?

  a. Are the findings discussed in the light of existing literature?

  b. Are conclusions justified by the findings?

  c. Have alternative explanations for the findings been explored and discounted?

10. To what extent are the findings of the study transferable to other settings?

  a. Were the subjects similar in important respects to those of interest to you?

  b. Was the context similar to or different from your own setting?

  c. How applicable are the findings to practice, policy or theoretical knowledge?

Appendix 4

Search structure template

Review question:

_____

① AND

② AND

③ AND

④

Appendix 5

Professional Capabilities Framework

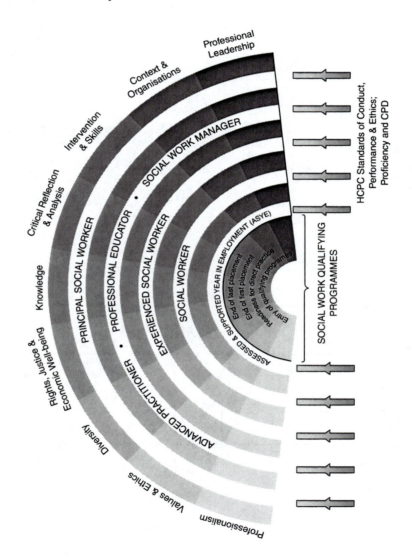

Professional Capabilities Framework diagram reproduced with permission of The College of Social Work

Glossary

Action research A reflective process of iterative problem solving in teams and organisations, usually focusing on a particular issue; such activity is more often termed a 'quality improvement process' now.

Attrition bias Bias in an experimental study caused by participants not completing the planned intervention. This can be a particular issue in studies of the effectiveness of social work interventions.

Audit See **Professional audit**.

Blinded, blinding See **Masked, masking**.

Boolean algebra When searching bibliographic databases the search terms are joined by operators (such as AND and OR) which specify how the search terms are to be treated. These operators work according to mathematical logic developed by George Boole (1815–64).

Case-control study A study design in which two groups which differ in terms of outcome are identified and then compared in terms of factors which may have led to these differences in outcome. Thus people who have some undesirable (i.e. ill-)health or social outcome are compared with people who are otherwise similar to seek to identify causes. The method is widely used in epidemiology, but deserves greater usage in social work (social epidemiology) to study risk factors.

Case study A detailed study of an individual person, family, group, team or organisation in its context so as to derive some knowledge from which generalisable lessons might be drawn. It is particularly useful where there is an unusual case of some problem; a case-law judgment; a pilot study in an organisation; and similar rare events.

Census Where data is gathered about all the members of a given population, by contrast to a **sample**.

Cross-sectional survey See **Survey**. This term is used to provide clarity where the term 'survey' is also being applied to longitudinal cohort studies.

Data Information collected for research, professional audit or service evaluation is called 'data'. These may be qualitative (words) or quantitative (numbers). The data may be obtained from questionnaires, files, electronic records, interviews, focus groups, observations, and through various measures such as indexes (e.g. socioeconomic status) or scales (e.g. measures of anxiety, depression, quality of life, social inclusion, stress, etc.)

Deductive research Research which proceeds by logical steps of deductive reasoning to reach a conclusion about the world (see also **Inductive research**).

Descriptive statistics Analysis of survey data that describes the sample from which data was gathered (see also **Inferential statistics**).

Effect size In any quantitative study this is a measure of the strength of a variable in which we are interested. In (quasi-)experimental studies, this is the size of the effect caused by the intervention of interest.

Empirical Derived from research, whether surveys or experiments or qualitative studies. In general reviews of evidence provide an overview of empirical research.

Ethnography The study of people in their 'natural' environment has led to a research method that focuses on observation of people in their cultural setting, whether domestic, at work, spiritual or recreational.

Evaluation See **Service evaluation**.

Evidence Knowledge produced by research, service evaluation and professional audit activities. The term 'evidence' also encompasses the message that evidence is tentative (rather than the product of immutable logic), may on occasions be misleading or contradicted by other research, and is part of a process of accumulation and synthesis to form a coherent body of knowledge.

Experimental study Where receipt of the intervention of interest is decided by the research team, participants are randomly allocated to the intervention under study with another group of participants not receiving this intervention (see also **Quasi-experimental study; Randomised controlled trial**).

Expert validation The validation of qualitative research by presenting the findings for comment to those with some expertise on the topic (see also **Respondent validation**).

External validity The extent to which the study findings may confidently be generalised to other people and situations (see also **Internal validity** and **Reliability**).

Fidelity See **Intervention fidelity**.

Findings The presentation of detailed data from a qualitative study (see also **Results**).

Focus group A method of data gathering in qualitative research where participants share ideas on the study topic with other participants with the aim of creating a richness of data through the interaction.

Grey literature Any publication that is not controlled by a commercial publisher. In practice, it is used to mean papers that are not reviewed by anonymous, 'masked' reviewers with expertise in the field. Grey literature includes conference papers, organisation reports and news-sheets, as well as theses and dissertations produced as part of academic studies.

Grounded theory A qualitative research design which emphasises generating new concepts and a new theoretical framework. The concept of 'saturation sampling' – continuing sampling until no substantive new themes emerge from the data – comes from grounded theory.

Hypothesis A statement about a relationship between two quantitative variables which is then tested through a survey or (quasi-)experimental study.

Incidence The frequency of occurrence of an event (such as referrals for a type of problem) during a specified time period (see also **Prevalence**).

Index-term searching Searching a bibliographic database using the thesaurus of terms on the database that has been used to index the abstracts (see also **Text-term searching**).

Inductive research Research which argues from a limited number of examples to general (theoretical) statements about the world (see also **Deductive research**).

Inferential statistics Analysis of survey data so as to make predictions about the entire population from which the sample studied is drawn (see also **Descriptive statistics**).

Internal validity The extent to which the measured effects of an intervention may confidently be ascribed to that intervention, which relates to avoidance of bias in the study design (see also **External validity; Reliability**).

Interpretative phenomenological analysis (IPA) A qualitative research design focusing on how a person makes sense of some aspect of their experience. In a social work context this is usually regarding their presenting problem or the process of recovery and growth through receipt of a service.

Interrupted time series (ITS) design A research design where multiple observations are made over a period of time, and where there are periods with and without the intervention of interest. This enables measures of the effects of the intervention.

Intervention fidelity In a (quasi-)experimental study of the effectiveness of an intervention, the faithfulness with which the intervention has been delivered. The intervention must be defined sufficiently clearly and any variations in how it is delivered must be within acceptable limits for the study to be meaningful and useful.

Interview See **Semi-structured interview**

Knowledge An understanding or explanation of a social phenomenon (such as client and family needs and the mechanisms of helping processes) based on research and theoretical understandings that are used to inform professional practice. *Knowledge involves gathering, analysing and synthesising different theories (explanations) to arrive at some kind of tentative understanding, hypothesis or judgement* (Trevithick, 2008, p3). An SCIE paper (Pawson et al., 2003) conceptualises social care knowledge as comprising organisational, practitioner, policy community and user and carer dimensions as well as research knowledge.

Literature mapping Providing an overview of types and subtopics of literature on a particular topic (see also **Systematic literature mapping**).

Longitudinal study A study that involves repeated measures of the same variables over time so as to identify correlations (see also **Cross-sectional survey**; **Survey**).

Masked, masking A process for reducing bias in experimental studies of effectiveness by ensuring that (1) participants do not know whether or not they are receiving the intervention; and sometimes also (2) those measuring outcomes are not aware of which trial group the participant they are measuring belongs to. The term is also sometimes called 'blinded' or 'blinding', although this terminology may be confusing where the study relates to visual impairment. The terms are also used in relation to peer-review of manuscripts submitted for publication in a journal, where the reviewers do not know the identity of the author(s).

Meta-analysis Combining the results of quantitative studies using statistical methods so as provide an overall estimate of effect (see **Experimental** and **Quasi-experimental studies**) or to identify patterns of correlation (see **Survey**).

Meta-ethnography Combining ethnographic studies using principles of **ethnography**.

Meta-synthesis Combining the findings of qualitative studies using principles of **qualitative research**.

Narrative review A review of research where, after some process of study selection, the results of studies, whether qualitative, quantitative or mixed methods, are combined in a narrative in terms of their main conclusions (see also **Narrative synthesis**; **Systematic narrative review**).

Narrative synthesis Combining the findings of studies, whether qualitative, quantitative or mixed methods, in a narrative in terms of their main conclusions.

Natural experiment Where the people (or more often clusters of people) receiving the intervention of interest are not determined by the research team, but where the process of allocation might be regarded as resembling random allocation. This can occur, for example, where a new type of intervention is introduced as a pilot in one geographical area but not another for reasons unconnected with the characteristics of the population. This provides a valuable opportunity for studying the effects of a social work intervention.

Organisational knowledge Generated through the management of services and the organisations that deliver them, including social care governance processes (Taylor and Campbell, 2011).

Performance bias Where the difference between experience of the intervention group and the control group is not just the planned intervention, thereby mitigating or enhancing the effect of the intervention itself. This may be due to the environment in which the intervention is conducted.

Population The totality of instances to which the research is to be generalised.

Prevalence The proportion of a population that has a particular characteristic, such as a problem of concern to social work (see also **Incidence**).

Probability sample The sampling approach generally used in survey research so as to gather data from a sample that is representative of the population to which the results are to be generalised. Every person in the population of interest has a chance of being selected as part of the sample (see also **Random sample**).

Professional audit Designed and conducted to produce information to inform delivery of best care by answering the question: 'Does this service reach a predetermined standard?' (Health Research Authority, 2013). Professional audit is clearly distinguished for governance purposes from **research** and from **service evaluation**, even though similar research methods may be used.

Purposive sample The sampling approach generally used in qualitative research whereby participants are selected 'for a purpose', essentially as being 'information-rich' in relation to the topic of the study – i.e. they have experienced what it is the researcher wants to study.

Qualitative research Data gathered in the form of language and most often, for the present purpose, through interviews or focus groups although observation and written data are also used. The aim is to understand social phenomena in their natural (including service delivery and work) settings.

Quantitative research Data gathered in the form of numbers whether in **surveys** or **experimental** or **quasi-experimental studies**, although **longitudinal** and **case-control studies** are also widely used. The aim is to measure social phenomena (including social needs, well-being and the effects of service provision) and the relationships between phenomena (such as factors that lead to higher risks or greater likelihood of benefiting from a particular intervention).

Quasi-experimental study Similar to an **experimental study** but where receipt of the intervention of interest is not assigned by the research team as part of a randomisation process.

Randomised controlled trial The classical **experimental** design, and best suited – where it is feasible – to measuring the effectiveness of an intervention. A group of people receiving the intervention are compared with similar people who do not receive the intervention, people having been allocated at random to the two groups.

Random sample The ideal sampling approach in survey research so as to gather data from a sample that is representative of the population to which the results are to be generalised. Every person in the population of interest has an equal chance of being selected as part of the sample (see also **Probability sample**).

Reliability The consistency of research measures, primarily in terms of whether similar results are obtained if the study is repeated (see also **Validity**).

Research Studies aiming to derive generalisable new knowledge including studies that aim to generate **hypotheses** (inductive, usually qualitative) as well as studies that aim to test hypotheses (surveys or experimental) (see Health Research Authority, 2013). Research is clearly distinguished for governance purposes from **service evaluation** and from **professional audit**, even though similar research methods may be used.

Respondent validation The validation of qualitative research by presenting the findings for comment to those who participated in the study (see also **Expert validation**).

Results The presentation of detailed data from a quantitative study (see also **Findings**).

Sample A subset of a **population** from which data is gathered in order to make some inference about the population as a whole.

Sampling The process of selecting the sources of data to be used in a **research, professional audit** or **service evaluation**.

Saturation sampling Within qualitative research the process expounded within **grounded theory** of continuing sampling until no new data relating to the theme is obtained, thereby providing a rich account of that construct in the **findings**.

Search formula A sequence of topic words joined by **Boolean** operators that are used in searching bibliographic databases to identify relevant journal articles. The search formula may include both **index-term** and **text-term searching**.

Secondary data Data that is collected by someone other than the researcher, such as organisational (client or staff) records, by contrast with primary data that is gathered by the researcher him- or herself.

Selection bias Bias due to the selection of individuals or other data for analysis not being random, whether in relation to a **survey** sample or in relation to allocation of participants to intervention and control arms of an **experimental** study (see also **Randomised controlled trial**).

Semi-structured interview A method of data gathering in qualitative research where participants have the opportunity to explore the topic of interest within the privacy of a one-to-one interview.

Service evaluation Designed and conducted to define or judge current care, to answer the question 'What standard does this service achieve?' (Health Research Authority, 2013). Service evaluation is clearly distinguished for governance purposes from research and from professional audit, even though similar research methods may be used.

Significance See **Statistical significance**.

Single subject design See **Case study**.

Single system design See **Case study**.

Standard deviation (σ) A measure of the dispersion of a set of data values.

Statistical significance The probability of the result not being due to chance. This may apply in relation to correlations between variables measured in a **survey**, or the measured effects of an intervention in an **experimental** or **quasi-experimental study**. This is measured primarily in terms of a p-value: the probability of observing the effect even though it is not attributable to the cause being studied.

Survey Gathering data at a point in time to study the prevalence or correlations of variables within a **population**. Survey data is gathered through questionnaires or using a data-extraction tool if the data is from files or similar records.

Synthesis Combining the findings of research, whether using **meta-analysis**, **meta-synthesis**, **narrative synthesis** or any other method that might have a specific name.

Systematic literature mapping A systematic approach using explicit methods for **literature mapping**. The distinction between the terms parallels the distinction between **narrative review** and **systematic narrative review**, so a systematic literature map will have an explicit and justifiable method for each stage of the process: (1) study identification; (2) quality appraisal; and (3) synthesis.

Systematic narrative review Where a **narrative synthesis** is part of a review that has an explicit and robust methodology for identification of relevant research or for quality appraisal of the research or both, but not for the synthesis, we use the term 'systematic narrative review'. Robust approaches to quality appraisal would be a waste of effort if the process of identifying relevant research were not robust, so in practice the term most commonly applies to reviews where there is a robust search methodology for identifying studies or for both of the two stages before synthesis. Systematic narrative reviews generally address questions of perspectives on care and professional processes, including both qualitative and quantitative studies on the topic, or more diffuse questions addressed by a variety of research designs.

Systematic review Where a review of research has an explicit and robust methodology for (1) identification of relevant research, (2) quality appraisal and (3) synthesis (i.e. **meta-analysis** or **meta-synthesis**) we use the term 'systematic review'. A systematic review may address a question of outcomes of an intervention, perspectives on care processes or best evidence on risk factors and thus may focus on (quasi-)experimental, qualitative or survey research but will not cross these major categories of research design.

Text-term searching Searching a bibliographic database for terms used by the author in the title or abstract of the article (see also **Index-term searching**).

Thematic analysis Analysis of qualitative data to identify patterns of meanings expressed by participants; their understandings of the world; and their rationalisations for behaviours.

User and carer knowledge User and carer knowledge is knowledge that comes directly from the experience of using a social care (including social work) service or being a primary carer (usually a family member) of someone who is using such a service.

Validity See **Internal validity** and **External validity**.

References

Agnew, A, Manktelow, R, Taylor, BJ and Jones, L (2010) Bereavement needs assessment in specialist palliative care settings: A review of the literature. *Palliative Medicine*, 24 (1): 46–59.

Atherton, C and Hodson, R (2006) Firm foundations: More than words – what must organizations do to support evidence-informed practice? SSRG Annual Workshop 2006 New Directions in Social Care: Meeting the Challenge of Change, March 27–29 2006, Oxford, England.

Austin, MJ, Dal Santo, TS and Lee, C (2012) Building organisational supports for research-minded practitioners. *Journal of Evidence-Based Social Work*, 9 (1–2): 174–211.

Barratt, M (2003) Organizational support for evidence-based practice within child and family social work: A collaborative study. *Child & Family Social Work*, 8 (2): 143–50.

Bates, S and Coren, E (2006) *SCIE Systematic Map Report 1: The extent and impact of parental mental health problems on families and the acceptability, accessibility and effectiveness of interventions.* Bristol: Social Care Institute for Excellence.

Begley, E, O'Brien, M, Carter-Anand, J, Killick, C and Taylor, B (2012) Older people's views of support services in response to elder abuse in communities across Ireland. *Quality in Ageing and Older Adults*, 13 (1): 48–59.

Bergman, EML (2012) Finding citations to social work literature: The relative benefits of using 'Web of Science', 'Scopus' or 'Google Scholar'. *Journal of Academic Librarianship*, 38 (6): 370–9.

Best, P, Taylor, BJ and Manktelow, R (2014a) Online communication, social media and adolescent well-being: A systematic narrative review. *Children and Youth Service Review*, 41: 27–36.

Best, P, Taylor, BJ, Manktelow, R and McQuilkin, J (2014b) Systematically retrieving research in the digital age: Case study on the topic of social networking sites and young people's mental health. *Journal of Information Science*, 40 (3): 346–56.

Bickman, L and Rog, DJ (eds) (2008) *The SAGE Handbook of Applied Social Research.* Thousand Oaks, CA: SAGE.

Biernacki, P (1986) *Pathways from Heroin Addiction: Recovery without treatment.* Philadelphia, PA: Temple University Press.

Bloom, M, Fischer, J and Orme, JG (2009) *Evaluating Practice: Guidelines for the accountable professional* (6th edition). Boston, MA: Allyn & Bacon.

Bolam v Friern Hospital Management Committee [1957] 1 WLR 582 (QB).

Bolitho v City and Hackney Health Authority [1998] AC 232 (HL).

Boote, J, Baird, W and Sutton, A (2011) Public involvement in the systematic review process in health and social care: A narrative review of case examples. *Health Policy*, 102 (2–3): 105–16.

Bostwick Jr, GJ and Kyle, NS (2011) Measurement. In: Grinnell Jr, RM and Unrau, YA (eds) *Social Work Research and Evaluation: Foundations of evidence-based practice* (9th edition) New York: Oxford University Press, 181–192.

Braun, V and Clarke, V (2006) Using thematic analysis in psychology. *Qualitative Research in Psychology*, 3 (2): 77–101.

Burns, S and Schubotz, D (2009) Demonstrating the merits of the peer research process: A Northern Ireland case study. *Field Methods*, 21 (3): 193–208.

Cable, V (2004) Does evidence matter? A transcript of a talk at Overseas Development Institute, 7 May 2003. London: Overseas Development Institute. Available at: www.odi.org/sites/odi.org.uk/files/odi-assets/publications-opinion-files/206.pdf

Campbell, A, Macdonald, G, Minozzi, S, Gardner, E and Taylor, BJ (2010) Cognitive behavioural therapy for substance abuse in young offenders (Protocol). *Cochrane Database of Systematic Reviews*, Issue 11. Art. No.: CD008801.

Campbell, A, Taylor, BJ and McGlade, A (2016) *Research Design in Social Work: Qualitative, quantitative and mixed methods*. London: SAGE.

Carpenter, J, Webb, C, Bostock, L and Coomber, C (2012) *Research Briefing 43: Effective supervision in social work and social care*. London: Social Care Institute for Excellence.

Centre for Reviews and Dissemination (2009) *Systematic Reviews: CRD's guidance for undertaking reviews in health care*. York: University of York.

Centre for Social Work and Social Care Research (2009) *Social Care Research Priorities and Capacity: Consultation exercise final report*. Swansea: Swansea University.

Chalmers, I and Altman, D (1995) *Systematic Reviews*. London: BMJ Publishing.

Charmaz, K (2006) *Constructing Grounded Theory: A practical guide through qualitative analysis*. New York: SAGE.

Chen, X (2006) MetaLib, WebFeat and Google: The strengths and weaknesses of federated search engines compared with Google. *Online Information Review*, 30 (4): 413–27.

Cochrane, AL (1972) *Effectiveness and Efficiency: Random reflections on the health service*. London: Nuffield Provincial Hospitals Trust.

Cochrane Effective Practice and Organisation of Care Group (EPOC). Available at: www.epoc.cochrane.org

Coffey, A and Atkinson, P (1998) *Making Sense of Qualitative Data: Complementary research strategies*. London: SAGE.

Coiera, E (2001) Maximising the uptake of evidence into clinical practice: An information economics approach. *Medical Journal of Australia*, 174 (9): 467–70.

Collins, E, and Daly, E (2011) *Decision Making and Social Work in Scotland: The role of evidence and practice wisdom*. Glasgow: Institute for Research and Innovation in Social Services.

Cooper, H (1998) *Synthesizing Research: A guide for literature reviews*. New York: SAGE.

Corbin, J and Strauss, AL (2008) *Basics of Qualitative Research: Techniques and procedures for developing grounded theory* (3rd edition). Thousand Oaks, CA: SAGE.

Coren, E and Fisher, M (2006) *The Conduct of Systematic Research Reviews for SCIE Knowledge Reviews.* London: Social Care Institute for Excellence.

Coulter, S (2011) Systemic family therapy for families who have experienced trauma: A randomised controlled trial. *British Journal of Social Work,* 41 (3): 502–19.

Covell, NH, McCorkle, BH, Weissman, EM, Summerfelt, T and Essock, SM (2007) What's in a name? Terms preferred by service recipients. *Administration and Policy in Mental Health,* 34: 443–7.

Critical Appraisal Skills Programme (CASP) (1998) *Appraising the Evidence.* Oxford: CASP. Available at: www.casp-uk.net/#!appraising-the-evidence/c23r5

Darragh, E and Taylor, BJ (2008) Research and reflective practice. In: Higham, P (ed.) *Post Qualifying Social Work Practice.* London: SAGE, 148–60.

Davidson, G, Devaney, J and Spratt, T (2010) The impact of adversity in childhood on outcomes in adulthood: Research lessons and limitations. *Journal of Social Work,* 10 (4): 369–90.

Deeks, JJ, Dinnes, J, D'Amico, R, Sowden, AJ, Sakarovitch, C, Song, F, Petticrew, M and Altman, DG (2003) Evaluating non-randomised intervention studies. *Health Technology Assessment,* 7(27): 1–179.

Department of Health (1998) *Modernising Health and Social Services: National priorities guidance,* 1999/00–2001/02. London: Department of Health.

Department of Health (2001) *Treatment Choice in Psychological Therapies and Counselling: Evidence based clinical practice guideline.* London: Department of Health.

De Vaus, D (2013) *Surveys in Social Research* (6th edition). London: Routledge.

Diggle, T, McConachie, HR and Randle, VRL (2002) Parent-mediated early intervention for young children with autism spectrum disorder. *The Cochrane Database of Systematic Reviews,* Issue 2. Art. No.: CD003496; doi: 10.1002/14651858.CD003496.

Dixon-Woods, M, Cavers, D, Agarwal, S, Annandale, E, Arthur, A, Harvey, J, Hsu, R, Katbamna, S, Olsen, R, Smith, L, Riley, R and Sutton, AJ (2006) Conducting a critical interpretive synthesis of the literature on access to healthcare by vulnerable groups. *BMC Medical Research Methodology,* 6 (35). Available at: www.biomedcentral.com/1471-2288/6/35

Downs, SH and Black, N (1998) The feasibility of creating a checklist for the assessment of the methodological quality of both randomised and non-randomised studies of healthcare interventions. *Journal of Epidemiology and Community Health,* 52 (6): 377–84.

Drury-Hudson, J (1999) Decision making in child protection: The use of theoretical, empirical and procedural knowledge by novices and experts and implications for fieldwork placement. *British Journal of Social Work,* 29 (1): 147–69.

Duffy, M, Gillespie, K and Clark, DM (2007) Post-traumatic stress disorder in the context of terrorism and other civil conflict in Northern Ireland: Randomised controlled trial. *British Medical Journal,* 334 (7604): 1147–50.

Economic and Social Research Council (2008) *Strategic Adviser for Social Work and Social Care Research: Commissioning brief.* Swindon: ESRC.

Elliot, R, Fisher, CT and Rennie, DL (1999) Evolving guidelines for publication of qualitative research studies in psychology and related fields. *British Journal of Clinical Psychology,* 38 (3): 215–29.

Engel, RJ and Schutt, RK (2012) *The Practice of Research in Social Work* (3rd edition). Thousand Oaks, CA: SAGE.

Everitt, BS, Landau, S and Morven, L (2001) *Cluster Analysis* (4th edition). New York: Oxford University Press.

Eysenck, HJ (1952) The effects of psychotherapy: An evaluation. *Journal of Consulting Psychology,* 16 (5): 319–24.

Falagas, ME, Pitsouni, EI, Malietzis, GA and Pappas, G (2007) Comparison of PubMed, Scopus, Web of Science, and Google Scholar: Strengths and weaknesses. *FASEB Journal,* 22 (2): 338–42.

Farrington, DP (2003) Methodological quality standards for evaluation research. *Annals of the American Academy of Political and Social Science,* 587 (1): 49–68.

Fetterman, DM (1998) *Ethnography* (2nd edition). London: SAGE.

Fischer, J (1973) Is social work effective? A review. *Social Work,* 18 (1): 5–20.

Fischer, J and Corcoran, K (2007a) *Measures for Clinical Practice and Research: A Sourcebook. Vol. 1: Couples, families, and children.* New York: Oxford University Press.

Fischer, J and Corcoran, K (2007b) *Measures for Clinical Practice and Research: A sourcebook. Vol. 2: Adults.* New York: Oxford University Press.

Fisher, M, Qureshi, H, Hardyman, W and Homewood, J (2006) *SCIE Report 09: Using qualitative research in systematic reviews: Older people's views of hospital discharge.* London: Social Care Institute for Excellence.

Fook, J (2000) Critical perspective on social work practice. In: O'Connor, I, Warburton, J and Smythe, P (eds) *Contemporary Perspectives on Social Work and the Human Services: Challenges and Change.* Melbourne: Addison Wesley Longman, 129–38.

Forbes, D, Forbes, SC, Blake, CM, Thiessen, EJ and Forbes, S (2015) Exercise programs for people with dementia. *Cochrane Database of Systematic Reviews,* Issue 4. Art. No.: CD006489.

Fowler, FJ (1995) *Improving Survey Questions: Design and evaluation.* New York: SAGE.

Fraser, MW, Day, SH, Galinsky, MJ, Hodges, VG and Smokowski, PR (2004) Conduct problems and peer rejection in childhood: A randomized trial of the Making Choices and Strong Families programs. *Research on Social Work Practice,* 14 (5): 313–24.

Friedlander, M and Ward, L (1984) Development and validation of the Supervisory Styles Inventory. *Journal of Counseling Psychology,* 31 (4): 541–57.

Gambrill, E (1999) Evidence-based practice: An alternative to authority-based practice. *Families in Society,* 80: 341–50.

Gambrill, E (2001) Social work: An authority-based profession. *Research on Social Work Practice,* 11 (2): 166–75.

Gee, JP (2005) *An Introduction to Discourse Analysis: Theory and method.* London: Routledge.

Gibbs, LE (1991) *Scientific Reasoning for Social Workers: Bridging the gap between research and practice.* New York: Macmillan.

Gibbs, LE (2003) *Evidence-based Practice for the Helping Professions: A practical guide with integrated multimedia.* Pacific Grove, CA: Brooks/Cole.

Gillespie, D (2014) Service evaluation of the positive living programmes in day centres. Dissertation (M.Sc. Professional Development in Social Work), University of Ulster.

Glass, GB, McGaw, B and Smith, ML (1981) *Meta-analysis in Social Research*. Beverley Hills, CA: SAGE.

Glass, GV (2000) *Meta-Analysis at 25*. Arizona State University College of Education. Available at: www.gvglass.info/papers/meta25.html

Hagan, R, Manktelow, R, Taylor, BJ and Mallett, J (2014) Reducing loneliness amongst older people: A systematic search and narrative review. *Aging and Mental Health*, 18 (6): 683–93.

Haight, WL (2010) The multiple roles of applied social science research in evidence-informed practice. *Social Work*, 55 (2): 101–3.

Hamilton, DJ, Taylor, BJ, Killick, C and Bickerstaff, D (2015) Suicidal ideation and behaviour among young people leaving care: Case-file survey. *Child Care in Practice*, 21 (2): 160–76.

Hanley, B, Bradburn, J, Barnes, M, Evans, C, Goodare, H, Kelson, M, Kent, A, Oliver, S, Thomas, S and Wallcraft, J (2004) *Involving the Public in NHS, Public Health, and Social Care Research: Briefing notes for researchers*. Eastleigh: INVOLVE.

Harrison, C and Humphreys, C (1998) *Keeping Research in Mind: Final report and recommendations for future development of social work education and training*. London: Central Council for Education and Training in Social Work.

Harvey, M (2014) Creating a journal club in a dementia home support team. Unpublished presentation at Decisions, Assessment, Risk and Evidence in Social Work Seminar, 20 November, Belfast, Northern Ireland.

Hayes, D and Devaney, J (2004) Accessing social work case files for research purposes: Some issues and problems. *Qualitative Social Work*, 3 (3): 313–33.

Health and Social Care Board (HSCB) (2015) *Social Work Research and Continuous Improvement Strategy 2015–2020: In pursuit of excellence in evidence informed practice in Northern Ireland*. Belfast: Health and Social Care Board.

Health Research Authority (2013) *Defining Research*. London: Health Research Authority.

Heffernan, K (2006) Social work, new public management and the language of 'service user'. *British Journal of Social Work*, 36: 139–47.

Henry, JD, Thompson, C, Ruffman, T, Leslie, F, Withall, A, Sachdev, P and Brodarty, H (2009) Threat perception in mild cognitive impairment and early dementia. *Journals of Gerontology. Series B, Psychological Sciences and Social Sciences*, 64 (5): 603–7.

Henry, JD, Thompson, C, Ruffman, T, Leslie, F, Withall, A, Sachdev, P and Brodaty, H (2009) Threat perception in mild cognitive impairment and early dementia. *The Journals of Gerontology: Series B: Psychological Sciences and Social Sciences*, 64B (5): 603–7; doi: 10.1093/geronb/gbp064.

Hodson, R (2003) *Leading the Drive for Evidence Based Practice in Services for Children and Families: Summary report of a study conducted for research in practice*. Totnes: Research in Practice.

Hoole, L and Morgan, S (2011) 'It's only right that we get involved': Service-user perspectives on involvement in learning disability services. *British Journal of Learning Disabilities*, 39 (1): 5–10.

Houston, S (2015) *Reflective Practice: A model for supervision and practice in social work*. Belfast: Northern Ireland Social Care Council.

Howard, MO, McMillen, CJ and Pollio, DE (2003) Teaching evidence-based practice: Toward a new paradigm for social work education. *Research on Social Work Practice,* 13 (2): 234–59.

Howell, WS (1982) *The Empathic Communicator.* Belmont, CA: Wadsworth.

Humphries, B (2003) What else counts as evidence in evidence-based social work? *Social Work Education,* 22 (1): 81–91.

Institute for Research and Innovation in Social Services (IRISS) (2008) *Towards a Research and Development Strategy for Social Services in Scotland.* Scotland: Institute for Research and Innovation in Social Services.

International Association of Schools of Social Work (2001) Global definition of social work. Available at: http://ifsw.org/get-involved/global-definition-of-social-work/

INVOLVE (2010) *Good Practice in Active Public Involvement in Research.* Eastleigh: National Institute for Health Research. Available at: www.rds-london.nihr.ac.uk/RDSLondon/media/RDSContent/files/PDFs/Good-practice-in-active-public-involvement-in-research.pdf

Jensen, J, Lundin-Olsson, L, Nyberg, L and Gustafson, Y (2002) Fall and injury prevention in older people living in residential care facilities: A cluster randomized trial. *Annals of Internal Medicine,* 136 (10): 733–41.

Joint University Council Social Work Education Committee (JUCSWEC) (2006) *A Social Work Research Strategy in Higher Education 2006–2020.* London: Social Care Workforce Research Unit.

Keaney, F, Strang, J, Martinez-Raga, J, Spektor, D, Manning, V, Kelleher, M, Wilson-Jones, C, Wanagaratne, S and Sabater, A (2004) Does anyone care about names? How attendees at substance misuse services like to be addressed by professionals. *European Addiction Research,* 10: 75–9.

Killick, C (2005) DipSW students' satisfaction with practice teaching on their first placement. *Journal of Practice Teaching and Learning,* 6 (1): 39–56.

Killick, C and Taylor, BJ (2009) Professional decision making on elder abuse: Systematic narrative review. *Journal of Elder Abuse and Neglect,* 21 (3): 211–38.

Killick, C, Taylor, BJ, Begley, E, Anand, JC and O'Brien, M (2015) Older people's conceptualization of abuse: A systematic narrative review. *Journal of Elder Abuse and Neglect,* 27 (2): 100–20.

Kitson, A, Harvey, G and McCormack, B (1998) Enabling the implementation of evidence based practice: A conceptual framework. *Quality in Health Care,* 7: 149–58.

Knapp, M (2007) Why do we spend so much on health care when social care is the real challenge of an ageing population? *Journal of Health Services Research and Policy,* 12 (3): 192.

Kolb, DA, and Fry, RE (1974) *Toward an Applied Theory of Experiential Learning.* Boston, MA: Alfred P. Sloan School of Management.

Krysik, JL and Finn, J (2013) *Research for Effective Social Work Practice* (3rd edition). New York: Routledge.

Lave, J and Wenger, E (1991) *Situated Learning: Legitimate peripheral participation.* New York: Cambridge University Press.

Layard, R, Clark, D, Knapp, M and Mayraz, G (2007) Cost-benefit analysis of psychological therapy. *National Institute Economic Review,* 202 (1): 90–8.

Light, RJ and Smith, PV (1971) Accumulating evidence: Procedures for resolving contradictions among different research studies. *Howard Educational Review,* 41 (4): 429–71.

Lins, S, Hayder-Beichel, D, Rücker, G, Motschall, E, Antes, G, Meyer, G and Langer, G (2014) Efficacy and experiences of telephone counselling for informal carers of people with dementia. *Cochrane Database of Systematic Reviews,* Issue 9. Art. No.: CD009126.

Lipsey, MW and Wilson, DB (2001) *Practical Meta-analysis.* Thousand Oaks, CA: SAGE.

Lloyd, C, King, R, Bassett, H, Sandland, S and Saviage, G (2001) Patient, client or consumer: A survey of preferred terms. *Australasian Psychiatry,* 9: 321–4.

Lundahl, B, Yaffe, J and Hobson, J (2008) Today's studies, tomorrow's meta-analyses: Implications for evidence informed decision-making in social work. *Journal of Social Service Research,* 35 (1): 1–9.

MacAteer, A, Manktelow, R and Fitzsimons, L (2015) Mental health workers' perception of role self-efficacy and the organisational climate regarding the ethos of recovery. *British Journal of Social Work,* Advance Access; doi: 10.1093/bjsw/bcv054.

MacAuley, D, McCrum, E and Brown, C (1998) Randomised controlled trial of the READER method of critical appraisal in general practice. *British Medical Journal,* 316 (7138): 134–7.

Macdonald, G (2000) *Effective Interventions for Child Abuse.* Chichester: John Wiley & Sons.

Macdonald, G (2003) *Using Systematic Reviews to Improve Social Care.* London: Social Care Institute for Excellence.

Macdonald, G (2008) The evidence-based perspective. In: Davies, M (ed.) *The Blackwell Companion to Social Work* (3rd edition). Oxford: Blackwell.

Macdonald, G and Millen, S (2012) *Therapeutic Approaches to Social Work in Residential Child Care Settings.* London: Social Care Institute of Excellence.

Macdonald, G, Sheldon, B and Gillespie, J (1992) Contemporary studies of the effectiveness of social work. *British Journal of Social Work,* 22 (6): 615–43.

Marmot, MG (2004) Evidence based policy or policy based evidence. *British Medical Journal,* 328 (7445): 906–7.

Marsh, P and Fisher, M in collaboration with Mathers, N and Fish, S (2005) *Developing the Evidence Base for Social Work and Social Care Practice: Using knowledge in social care, report 10.* London: Social Care Institute for Excellence.

Martin, S, Kelly, G, Kernohan, WG, McCreight, B and Nugent, C (2008) Smart home technologies for health and social care support. *Cochrane Database of Systematic Reviews,* Issue 4. Art. No.: CD006412; doi: 10.1002/14651858. CD006412.pub2.

Mathiesen, S and Hohman, M (2013) Revalidation of an evidence-based practice scale for social work. *Journal of Social Work Education,* 49 (3): 451–60.

McColl, E, Jacoby, A, Thomas, L, Scoutter, J, Bamford, C, Steen, N, Thomas, R, Harvey, E, Garratt, A and Bond, J (2001) Design and use of questionnaires: A review of best practice applicable to surveys of health service staff and patients. *Health Technology Assessment,* 5 (31). Available at: www. journalslibrary.nihr.ac.uk/__data/assets/pdf_file/0006/64833/FullReport-hta5310.pdf

McDonald, A (2010) The impact of the 2005 Mental Capacity Act on social workers' decision making and approaches to the assessment of risk. *British Journal of Social Work,* 40 (4): 1229–46.

McFadden, P, Taylor, BJ, Campbell, A and McQuilkin, J (2012) Systematically identifying relevant research: Case study on child protection social workers' resilience. *Research on Social Work Practice,* 22 (6): 626–36.

McFadden, P, Campbell, A and Taylor, BJ (2015) Resilience and burnout in child protection social work: Individual and organizational themes from a systematic literature review. *British Journal of Social Work,* 45 (5): 1546–63; doi: 10.1093/bjse/bct210.

McGinn, AH, Taylor, BJ, McColgan, M and McQuilkin, J (2014) Social work literature searching: Current issues with databases and online search engines. *Research on Social Work Practice,* Advance Access. Available at: http://rsw.SAGEpub.com/content/early/2014/09/17/1049731514549423.full.pdf+html

McKenna, H, Cutliffe, J and McKenna, P (1999) Evidence-based practice: Demolishing some myths. *Nursing Standard,* 14 (16): 39–42.

McLaughlin, H (2006) Involving young service users as co-researchers: Possibilities, benefits and costs. *British Journal of Social Work,* 36 (8): 1395–410.

McNeese, CA and Thyer, BA (2004) Evidence-based practice and social work. *Journal of Evidence-Based Social Work,* 1 (1): 7–25.

Medical Research Council (2008) *Developing and Evaluating Complex Interventions.* London: Medical Research Council.

Medical Research Council (2010) *Using Natural Experiments to Evaluate Population Health Interventions: Guidance for producers and users of evidence.* London: Medical Research Council.

Minkler, M and Wallerstein, N (2003) Review essay community-based research: Celebration and concern. Community-based participatory research for health. *Michigan Journal of Community Service Learning,* 9 (3): 69–74.

Munro, E (2008) *Effective Child Protection.* London: SAGE.

National Institute for Health and Care Excellence (NICE) (2005) *Post-traumatic Stress Disorder: The management of PTSD in adults and children in primary and secondary care.* Clinical Guideline 26. London: NICE.

National Institute for Health Research (2010) *Systematic Reviews: Knowledge to support evidence-informed health and social care.* London: National Institute for Health Research.

National Institute for Social Care and Health Research. Available from: www.nischr.org.uk/.

Newman, T and McDaniel, B (2005) Getting research into practice: Healing damaged attachment processes in infancy. *Child Care in Practice,* 11 (1): 81–90.

Newman, T and McNeish, D (2002) Promoting evidence based practice in a child care charity: The Barnardo's experience. *Social Work & Social Sciences Review,* 10 (1): 51–62.

Noblit, GW and Hare, RD (1988) *Meta-ethnography: Synthesising qualitative studies.* New York: SAGE.

Northern Ireland Social Care Council (2015) *Professional in Practice: The continuous professional development framework for social work.* Available at: www.niscc.info/index.php/education-for-our-training-providers/social-work-professional-development-pq

Nutley, S (2010) Evidence-informed practice: Using research to improve services for children and young people. Presentation at the Centre for Effective Services seminar series on Developing evidence informed practice for children and young people: The 'why and the what', October 2010.

Nutley, S, Walter, I and Davies, H (2009) Promoting evidence-based practice models and mechanisms from cross-sector review. *Research on Social Work Practice*, 19 (5): 552–9.

O'Cathain, A, Thomas, KJ, Drabble, SJ, Rudolph, A and Hewison, J (2013) What can qualitative research do for randomised controlled trials? A systematic mapping review. *British Medical Journal Open*, 3 (6).

O'Connor, R and Sheehy, N (2000) *Understanding Suicidal Behaviour*. Leicester: BPS Books.

Olthuis, JV, Watt, MC, Bailey, K, Hayden, JA and Stewart, SH (2015) Therapist-supported internet cognitive behavioural therapy for anxiety disorders in adults. *Cochrane Database of Systematic Reviews*, Issue 3. Art. No.: CD011565.

Osmond, J and O'Connor, I (2006) Use of theory and research in social work practice: Implications for knowledge-based practice. *Australian Social Work*, 59 (1): 5–19.

Pallant, J (2013) *SPSS Survival Manual: A step by step guide to data analysis using IBM SPSS (5th edition)*. Maidenhead: Open University Press.

Pawson, R, Boaz, A, Grayson, L, Long, A and Barnes, C (2003) *Types and Quality of Knowledge in Social Care: Knowledge review 3*. London: Social Care Institute for Excellence.

Petticrew, M and Roberts, H (2006) *Systematic Reviews in the Social Sciences: A practical guide*. Oxford: Blackwell.

Pinkerton, J (1998) The impact of research on policy and practice: A systematic perspective. In: Iwaniec, D and Pinkerton, J (eds) *Making Research Work: Promoting child care policy and practice*. Chichester: Wiley, 27–45.

Platt, D, (2014) Implementing evidence-based practice: An organisational perspective. *British Journal of Social Work*, 44 (4): 905–23.

Popay, J and Roen, K (2003) *Synthesis of Evidence from Research Using Diverse Study Designs: A preliminary review of methodological work*. London: Social Care Institute for Excellence.

Popay, J, Roberts, H, Sowden, A, Petticrew, M, Arai, L, Rodgers, M, Britten, N, Roen, K and Duffy, S (2006) *Guidance on the Conduct of Narrative Synthesis in Systematic Reviews: A product of the ESRC methods programme*. London: Economic and Social Research Council.

Pray, JE (1991) Respecting the uniqueness of the individual: Social work practice within a reflective model. *Social Work*, 36 (1): 80–5.

Richards, H and Emslie, C (2000) The 'doctor' or the 'girl from the University'? Considering the influence of professional roles on qualitative interviewing. *Family Practice*, 17 (1): 71–5.

Ritchie, J and Lewis, J (2003) *Qualitative Research Practice: A guide for social science students and researchers*. London: SAGE.

Roberts, AR and Yeaker, K (eds) (2006) *Foundations of Evidence-based Social Work Practice*. New York: Oxford University Press.

Rowley, J and Johnson, F (2013) Understanding trust formation in digital information sources: The case of Wikipedia. *Journal of Information Science*, 39 (4): 494–508.

Rubin, A and Bellamy, J (2012) *Practitioner's Guide to Using Research for Evidence-based Practice* (2nd edition). Hoboken, NJ: Wiley.

Rutter, D, Francis, J, Coren, E and Fisher, M (2010) *SCIE Research Resource 1: SCIE systematic research reviews: Guidelines (2nd edition)*. London: Social Care Institute for Excellence.

Sackett, DL, Rosenberg, WM, Gray, JA, Haynes, RB and Richardson, WS (1996) Evidence based medicine: What it is and what it isn't. *British Medical Journal*, 312 (7023): 71–2.

Sandelowski, M and Barroso, J (2007) *Handbook for Synthesising Qualitative Research*. New York: Springer.

Schön, DA (1983) *The Reflective Practitioner: How professionals think in action*. London: Temple Smith.

Schön, DA (1987) *Educating the Reflective Practitioner: Toward a new design for teaching and learning in the professions*. San Francisco, CA: Jossey-Bass.

Seal, M (2008) *Not About Us Without Us: Client involvement in supported housing*. Lyme Regis: Russell House.

Sellick, MM, Delaney, R and Brownlee, K (2002) The deconstruction of professional knowledge: Accountability without authority. *Families in Society*, 83 (5): 493–8.

Shaw, I, Arksey, H and Mullender, A (2004) *SCIE Report 11: ESRC research, social work and social care*. London: Social Care Institute for Excellence.

Sheldon, B (1999) Cognitive behavioural methods in social care: A look at the evidence. In: Stepney, P and Ford, D (eds) *Social Work Models, Methods and Theories: A framework for practice*. Lyme Regis: Russell House, 74–6.

Sheldon, B (2001) The validity of evidence-based practice in social work: A reply to Stephen Webb. *British Journal of Social Work*, 31 (5): 801–9.

Sheldon, B and Macdonald, GM (1999) *Research and Practice in Social Care: Mind the gap*. Exeter: Centre for Evidence-Based Social Services, University of Exeter.

Sheldon, B, Chilvers, R, Ellis, A, Moseley, A and Tierney, S (2005) A pre-post empirical study of the obstacles to, and opportunities for, evidence-based practice in social care. In Bilson, A (ed.) *Evidence-based Practice and Social Work*. London: Whiting & Birch, 11–50.

Shlonsky, A and Gibbs, L (2006) Will the real evidence-based practice please stand up? Teaching the process of evidence-based practice to the helping professions. In: Roberts, AR and Yeager, KR (eds) *Foundations of Evidence-based Social Work Practice*. New York: Oxford University Press, 103–21.

Shlonsky, A, Baker, TB and Fuller-Thomson, E (2011a) Using methodological search filters to facilitate evidence-based social work practice. *Clinical Social Work Journal*, 39 (4): 390–9.

Shlonsky, A, Noonan, E, Littell, JH and Montgomery, P (2011b) The role of systematic reviews and the Campbell Collaboration in the realization of evidence-informed practice. *Clinical Social Work Journal*, 39 (4): 362–8.

Sinclair, R and Jacobs, C (1994) *Research in Personal Social Services: The experiences of three local authorities*. London: National Children's Bureau.

Smith, E, Donovan, S, Beresford, P, Manthorpe, J, Brearley, S, Sitzia, J and Ross, F (2009) Getting ready for user involvement in a systematic review. *Health Expectations*, 12 (2): 197–208.

Smith, GCS and Pell, JP (2003) Parachute use to prevent death and major trauma related to gravitational challenge: Systematic review of randomised controlled trials. *British Medical Journal*, 327 (7429): 1459–61.

Smith, JA (1999) Identity development during the transition to motherhood. *Journal of Reproductive and Infant Psychology*, 17 (3): 281–99.

Smith, JA, Flowers, P and Larkin, M (2009) *Interpretative Phenomenological Analysis: Theory, method and research*. London: SAGE.

Smith, ML and Glass, GV (1977) Meta-analysis of psychotherapy outcome studies. *American Psychologist*, 32 (9): 752–60.

Social Care Institute for Excellence (SCIE). Available at: www.scie.org.uk.

Soydan, H and Palinkas, L (2014) *Evidence-based Practice in Social Work: Development of a new professional culture*. London: Routledge.

Spencer, L, Ritchie, J, Lewis, J and Dillon, L (2003) *Quality in Qualitative Evaluation: A framework for assessing research evidence*. London: Her Majesty's Stationery Office.

Starks, H and Trinidad, SB (2007) Choose your method: A comparison of phenomenology, discourse analysis, and grounded theory. *Qualitative Health Research*, 17 (10): 1372–80.

Stevens, M, Liabo, K, Frost, S and Roberts, H (2005) Using research in practice: A research information service for social care practitioners. *Child & Family Social Work*, 10 (1): 67–75.

Stevenson, M, Taylor, BJ and McDowell, M (2014) Concepts for communication about risk in dementia care: Review (unpublished paper). Coleraine: Ulster University.

Strauss, A and Corbin, J (1998) *Basics of Qualitative Research: Techniques and procedures for developing grounded theory* (2nd edition). Thousand Oaks, CA: SAGE.

Taylor, BJ (2003) Literature searching. In: Miller, R and Brewer, J (eds) *The A to Z of Social Research*. London: SAGE, 171–6.

Taylor, BJ (2004) Risk in community care: Professional decision making on the long term care of older people (Ph.D. thesis), Queen's University Belfast.

Taylor, BJ (2006a) Factorial surveys: Using vignettes to study professional judgement. *British Journal of Social Work*, 36 (7): 1187–207.

Taylor, BJ (2006b) Risk management paradigms in health and social services for professional decision making on the long-term care of older people. *British Journal of Social Work*, 36 (8): 1411–29.

Taylor, BJ (2009) Invited commentary on papers by Holden et al. and Shek on the quality of Social Work Abstracts. *Research on Social Work Practice*, 19 (3): 366–9.

Taylor, BJ (ed.) (2011) *Working with Aggression and Resistance in Social Work*. London: SAGE.

Taylor, BJ (2012a) Intervention research. In: Gray, M, Midgley, J and Webb, S (eds) *Social Work Handbook*. New York: SAGE, 424–39.

Taylor, BJ (2012b) Developing an integrated assessment tool for the health and social care of older people. *British Journal of Social Work,* 42 (7): 1293–314.

Taylor, BJ (2013) *Professional Decision Making and Risk in Social Work* (2nd edition). London: SAGE.

Taylor, BJ (2016) Selecting your method. In: Campbell, A, Taylor, BJ and McGlade, A (eds) *Research Design in Social Work: Qualitative, quantitative and mixed methods.* London: SAGE, chapter 3.

Taylor, BJ and Campbell, B (2011) Quality, risk and governance: Social workers' perspectives. *International Journal of Leadership in Public Services,* 7 (4): 256–72.

Taylor, BJ and Donnelly, M (2006a) Professional perspectives on decision making about the long-term care of older people. *British Journal of Social Work,* 36 (5): 807–26.

Taylor, BJ and Donnelly, M (2006b) Risks to home care workers: Professional perspectives. *Health, Risk & Society,* 8 (3): 239–56.

Taylor, BJ and Killick, CJ (2013) Threshold decisions in child protection: Systematic narrative review of theoretical models used in empirical studies (conference abstract). *Medical Decision Making,* 33 (2): E145–E203.

Taylor, BJ, Dempster, M and Donnelly, M (2003) Hidden gems: Systematically searching electronic databases for research publications for social work and social care. *British Journal of Social Work,* 33 (4): 423–39.

Taylor, BJ, McGilloway, S and Donnelly, M (2004) Preparing young adults with disability for employment. *Health & Social Care in the Community,* 12 (2): 93–101.

Taylor, BJ, Dempster, M and Donnelly, M (2007a) Grading gems: Appraising the quality of research for social work and social care. *British Journal of Social Work,* 37 (2): 335–54.

Taylor, BJ, Wylie, E, Dempster, M and Donnelly, M (2007b) Systematically retrieving research: A case study evaluating seven databases. *Research on Social Work Practice,* 17 (6): 697–706.

Taylor, BJ, Mullineux, JC and Fleming, G (2010) Partnership, service needs and assessing competence in post qualifying education and training. *Social Work Education,* 29 (5): 475–89.

Taylor, BJ, Killick, C, O'Brien, M, Begley, E and Carter-Anand, J (2014) Older people's conceptualization of elder abuse and neglect. *Journal of Elder Abuse and Neglect,* 26 (3), 223–43; doi: 10.1080/08946566.2013.795881.

Tew, J, Gould, N, Abankwa, D, Barnes, H, Beresford, P, Carr, S, Copperman, J, Ramon, S, Rose, D, Sweeney, A and Woodward, L (2006) *Values and Methodologies for Social Research in Mental Health.* London: Social Care Institute for Excellence.

The College of Social Work (TCSW) (2012) *Professional Capabilities Framework.* London: The College of Social Work.

Thomas, J, Harden, A, Oakley, A, Sutcliffe, K, Rees, R, Brunton, G and Kavanagh, J (2004) Integrating qualitative research with trials in systematic reviews. *British Medical Journal,* 328 (7446): 1010–12.

Thornicroft, G, Rose, D, Huxley, P, Dale, G and Wykes, T (2002) What are the research priorities of mental health service users? *Journal of Mental Health,* 11 (1): 1–3.

Thyer, BA (ed.) (2010) *The Handbook of Social Work Research Methods* (2nd edition). Thousand Oaks, CA: SAGE.

Tozer, CL and Ray, S (1999) 20 questions: The research needs of children and family social workers. *Research, Policy and Planning,* 17 (1): 7–15.

Trevithick, P (2008) Revisiting the knowledge base of social work: A framework for practice. *British Journal of Social Work,* 38 (6): 1212–37.

Walsh, J and Boyle, J (2009) Improving acute psychiatric hospital services according to inpatient experiences. A user-led piece of research as a means to empowerment. *Issues in Mental Health Nursing,* 30 (1): 31–8.

Walsh, D and Downe, S (2005) Meta-synthesis method for qualitative research: A literature review. *Journal of Advanced Nursing,* 50 (2): 204–11.

Walter, I, Nutley, S, Percy-Smith, J, McNeish, D and Frost, S (2004) *Knowledge Review 7: Improving the use of research in social care practice.* London: Social Care Institute for Excellence.

Webber, M and Currin Salter, L (2011) Gearing practitioners up for research: Evaluation of a pilot online research training course for social workers. *Research Policy and Planning,* 28 (3): 185–97.

Weiss, CH (1979) The many meanings of research utilization. *Public Administration Review,* 39 (5): 426–31.

Weissman, MM and Sanderson, WC (2002) Problems and promises in modern psychotherapy: The need for increased training in evidence based treatments. In: Hamburg, B (ed.) *Modern Psychiatry: Challenges in educating health professionals to meet new needs.* New York: Josiah Macy Foundation, 132–60.

Wells, K and Littell, JH (2009) Study quality assessment in systematic reviews of research on intervention effects. *Research on Social Work Practice,* 19 (1): 52–62.

Wilson, G and Douglas, H (2007) Developing a culture of evidence-based practice in social work agencies in Northern Ireland. *Practice: Social Work in Action,* 19 (1): 19–32.

Wilson, P, Richardson, R, Sowdon, A and Evans, D (2001) Stage III phase 9: Getting evidence into practice. In: Khan, K, Riet, G, Glanville, J, Sowden, A and Kleijnen, J (eds) *Undertaking Systematic Reviews of Research on Effectiveness: CRD's guidance for those carrying out or commissioning reviews. CRD report 4* (2nd edition). York: NHS Centre for Reviews and Dissemination, University of York.

Winokur, M, Holtan, A and Batchelder, K (2014) Kinship care for the safety, permanency, and well-being of children removed from the home for maltreatment: A systematic review. *Campbell Systematic Reviews,* 10 (2). Available at: www.campbellcollaboration.org/lib/project/51/

Woods, B, Spector, AE, Jones, CA, Orrell, M and Davies, SP (2005) Reminiscence therapy for dementia. *Cochrane Database of Systematic Reviews,* Issue 2. Art. No.: CD001120.

Index